Nelli's Journey

Nelli's Journey

From the Depths of Evil to Reconciliation and Beyond

by

Nina Kaleska

DORRANCE PUBLISHING CO., INC.
PITTSBURGH, PENNSYLVANIA 15222

ISBN # 0-8059-6930-6
Printed in the United States of America

First Printing

For information or to order additional books, please write:
Dorrance Publishing Co., Inc.
701 Smithfield Street
Third Floor
Pittsburgh, Pennsylvania 15222
U.S.A.
1-800-788-7654

Or visit our web site and on-line catalog at
www.dorrancebookstore.com

To the memory of my beloved parents and sister
And to my sons, Ronald and Edward Harris,
the reason for my survival
and to the next generation, my grandchildren
Jeffrey and Laura

And with appreciation to my stepson,
Philip B. Auerbach,
for his devotion
And for his encouragement of my writing

Contents

Introduction

The Dream

In June of 1943, I was fourteen. I was lying on the top bunk in the barrack designated for the Aryan inmates. I don't remember how I got here. Martha, with the help of another "nurse", smuggled me into this place. I was very ill and barely able to walk. It was probably typhoid, but who knew?

In this barrack, the selections were only held for the almost dead. The doctor would come, inspect the inmates, jot down the tattooed number, and walk away. Martha covered me with layers of clothing, removed from dead inmates, to conceal my emaciated body and to make me look heavier and healthier. Every morning, Dr. Klein, one of the Nazi camp doctors, inspected his domain, and in the process this morning, he jotted down my tattooed number. We all knew what that meant. The trucks would remove the inmates and transport them to the gas chamber that evening. I was resolved to my fate. I was too weak to care.

I fell into a deep sleep. As though in some eerie mist, everything around me appeared in slow motion. I was walking on a high mountaintop that led toward a deep gorge. I was aware that if I continued to walk, I would fall from the dangerously steep precipice, but I experienced no fear and continued to walk. My hair was blowing in the wind. That seemed odd because at that time, all my hair had been shaved off. And in reality, I was also too weak to walk. I was hopping and smiling with a feeling of strange joy. I kept walking closer toward the precipice.

Suddenly, someone grabbed me by the arm and I woke up. I didn't know if I was still dreaming or if this was reality; I was delirious with fever. When I opened my eyes, I saw Martha standing over me, her face covered with tears. She took me in her arms and whispered, "My darling, Nellinka, a miracle just happened. The Aryan doctor in this barrack persuaded Dr. Klein to remove your number from his pad, marking your removal. You will not be taken away tonight."

Adjacent to my bunk laid a lady with whom I talked over the past few days. In this place, a few days was considered an eternity. She told me that she was a psychotherapist and had studied with Sigmund Freud. I did not know what the word psychotherapist meant. And I had no idea who Freud was. She was sent to this camp because her father was Jewish.

I told her my strange dream. What she told me was so striking that I remember the conversation with total clarity to this day. "This is amazing," she explained. "You have actually seen and predicted your own future. This does not often happen except on rare occasions under deep analysis." I did not understand what she was saying to me. For the brief time we "knew" each other, she was so willing to talk to me about many subjects, many subjects I knew nothing about. I relished my conversations with her. A few days later, she died. I knew her name was Adele, and I grieved for her....

Chapter 1

Grodno

I was born in Grodno, Poland in 1929. Grodno is located in the Northeast part of Poland. We were a small family: my parents, my older sister Sala and I. Sala was five years older than I. Our parents created a comfortable and pleasant home filled with caring and love. Sala was the athlete in the family: a champion gymnast, ice skater, and swimmer. I admired and adored her. She was very popular, and our home was often full of her devoted friends.

Sadly, I now have only vague recollections of my father. No photos of him remain. My father was a specialist in trees, and his work took him mainly to the extensive forests around our town of Grodno and around other parts of eastern Poland. I loved riding with him occasionally on his chestnut-colored horse, and in the cold winters, he would cover me with a blanket. He always wore a leather jacket, a leather cap and boots, and he looked robust, healthy, and handsome. He seemed more sunburned in winter than in summer because of the strong winds and reflections off the deep snow. During winters, my father would often take my sister and me sledding and ice-skating. I loved being with him.

My four grandparents had all died before I was born, and my father's relatives mostly lived in other towns. We didn't see them very often.

My mother was more the intellect and the artist. She had a beautiful singing voice. Music constantly filled our home with singing, guitar playing, piano playing, and the radio. I gravitated naturally to music. I took ballet and piano lessons, and in school, I was always picked as a soloist in the school chorus.

Although my sister and I went to public schools for most of our youth, for about two years, we attended a Catholic school because education was very important to my parents and that school was considered the best in town. And when most of the students attended catechism classes, the five Jewish children in the school had their own religious instructions.

Academically, I was pretty bad at math, which I simply did not enjoy, but I did well in history, geography, literature, and languages. In addition to Polish, we studied Latin and later started French.

My normal, comfortable, and innocent childhood suddenly ended in 1939 when I was ten. Hitler and Stalin had made a non-aggression pact that divided Poland in half, and our half was suddenly annexed to the USSR as part of what was then Belyorussia and what is now Belarus.

Within a short time, everything changed. When we returned to school, many new courses were in Russian; the new textbooks and the curriculum were Soviet; and a picture of Papa Stalin prominently hung in all the classrooms. I was soon inducted into the "Young Pioneers," wore a red scarf around my neck, and pledged allegiance to the glory of the Soviet Union. My parents must have been horrified—although they had no choice in the matter.

Since languages came easily to me, I learned Russian very quickly. We were taught devotion to building the Soviet motherland, devoid of differences between classes, peoples, or religions. The Soviet teachers were always on the lookout for early signs of emerging talent in their pupils. Sala, of course, was an athlete. And the teachers told my mother that while my academics were nothing particularly stellar, they would certainly watch and cultivate my musical abilities.

My Mother – Rachil Kalecka

My sister Sala in 1939

Two years later in 1941, Sala and I were chosen to represent our school, leading it to the next stage in a national student competition held in Bialystok. Sala competed in all around gymnastics, and I in the choirs as a vocal soloist. That train trip was the first time I had been away so far from home, and it was very exciting to travel with all the older students. The return trip from Bialystok, however, was far different; a large number of the passengers were men in military uniforms, and general chaos seemed to prevail. We quickly learned that Hitler had broken his pact with Stalin and was invading eastern Poland. Our parents had largely shielded us from events catapulting in the outside world. Now those events came crashing into our reality.

When our train reached Grodno, the German bombs began to fall. We rushed home to our apartment, where our parents whisked us into an underground bunker.

And when we emerged, a huge and frightening Nazi tank was parked in the courtyard. My carefree, innocent world and childhood fun had vanished forever....

Chapter 2

The Abyss

Upon their conquest of eastern Poland in June 1941, the Germans wasted little time in initiating the Master Plan for the "Final Solution"—the total destruction of the Jewish people...

First, we were not allowed to walk on the sidewalks. Then we had to wear a yellow band, and then a blue Star of David was added. Our homes were vandalized with regularity; objects of great sentimentality and value were broken playfully by any German soldier who wanted a little fun. Brutality rampaged. I saw people being clubbed to death right in front of our home.

By November 1941, two ghettos were formed in Grodno. We left our homes for the last time, taking with us only the scantiest belongings. We were placed in Ghetto No. 2. My parents, my sister Sala, and I shared one room. Father went to work in the ghetto every day, and Sala and I attended an improvised school, hoping that we still might need an education.

We lived this way until suddenly, one Sunday in November 1942, and without any warning, everyone was rounded up. Less than one-third was marched off to Ghetto No. 1; the rest were evacuated the next day. My sister and I became separated from our parents. That Sunday in November was the last time we saw them. They left on the transport from Grodno. We had no idea where they were being taken.

During the time we lived in Ghetto No. 1, Sala and I both worked in a tobacco factory, returning at night to our little corner in the ghetto. The house in which we lived had belonged to a friend of mine. That family had already been evacuated. Many transports left Grodno during those few months, and each time Sala and I evaded them by hiding in different places: in the attic of our synagogue, behind a deep pile of snow, inside closets... I am glad we were slender in those days! We somehow managed to be optimistic about our future, and we both kidded each other. This attitude helped, even more so in later months when life really became unbearable.

On the morning of January 20th 1943, the sun shone so brightly that the snow looked even whiter than it had a right to be, and the weather was bitter cold. But on that day, our clever evasions ended. We were rounded up by screaming German guards with fierce growling dogs, whistles, and rubber batons that were used very freely. We were marched through the town to the railway station and shoved into cattle cars for what was to be a nightmare journey.

Many people died before we reached our unknown destination. They were the lucky ones. We were very cramped and had no sanitation facilities, water, or food—or so little that the rations were gone by the first day. I kept thinking of times when my mother would make me eat, and I would simply not be hungry. Perhaps I required less than others because I was so thin and never ate much. The stench inside the train was unbearable, and it was probably the worst part of that trip, at least for me.

We finally stepped off the train onto a newly created platform, specially built to welcome the human cargo. The fact that the wind and cold hit me in the face became the only nice part of this ordeal just beginning. The name Auschwitz was clearly written on a sign. Little did I know what that name would come to mean to me. The devil in his wildest imagination could not have conceived anything like this inferno on earth.

The Nazis, I learned years later, had built detention camps, prisoner camps, and work camps, all for those specific purposes.

This place was an extermination camp, created purposefully and literally for the destruction of European Jewry. It had Christian inmates, but they were usually there for political, criminal or prostitution charges. And the Christian inmates of Auschwitz were not subjected to the same treatment as the Jews.

The date of our arrival was January 24th 1943. I was to remain in that hell for twenty-four months—two whole years.

At the railway station, a selection was held. Out of 2,500 people on our train, 2,290 were sent immediately to the gas chambers. There were four crematoria, and sometimes, when the human load was heavy, victims were also burned in open graves. We spotted the flames but did not know then what they were. We were soon to find out.

The remaining 210 people from our transport consisted of 125 men and 85 women who were chosen to go into the camp. My first miracle happened when my sister, having noticed the smaller group of the selection, pushed me toward it and then followed. She was woman No. 85. I was wearing my mother's long coat that covered my young face and masked the fact that I was fourteen. Usually the people taken into the camp were between eighteen and thirty five. Only the young and the strong were acceptable. They didn't stay young or strong for very long.

As we marched off, we passed the gate on which were marked words that I did not understand then. It read in German: "Arbeit Macht Frei" (Work will liberate you). What irony!

We were taken to a building where we had to undress. Our few personal belongings were torn to shreds. Our heads were shaven, and a very large number was tattooed onto my left arm. It was very painful, and my sister, knowing my fear of doctors, whispered for me to have courage. A triangle was then tattooed underneath the number. That indicated that I was Jewish. I had long blond hair and blue eyes, making me look the perfect Aryan, and the woman who was executing her task questioned my race... as did Dr. Mengele later. My number was 31386. Sala's was 31387. From that moment on, I ceased to be a human being. We were told that originally they were going to tattoo us on the forehead, but apparently it was too difficult.

We were given clothing of dead Russian war prisoners, and we were grateful for its warmth. Then we went to our blocks. The first impression was of a large, barren barrack with boxes— great stretches of three-tiered wooden boxes—six feet wide, about three feet high, each accommodating between six to ten inmates and tremendously overcrowded. We were given horribly tasting food that I could barely swallow, in spite of my hunger. I soon got used to it. The food consisted of some kind of thin soup, bread, margarine, and sausage twice a week. We were then counted, yelled at, and shoved into these so-called sleeping quarters for the night. Thus began two years of indescribable hell for me.

The bunks were so overcrowded that it was impossible to turn around when sleeping. Usually someone died during the night. We hoped that the bunk space would remain empty, but it was soon occupied by another unfortunate inmate. Sooner or later, we were all assigned to carry dead bodies from the barracks to the outside wall. I washed my hands with tears that were flowing freely from my eyes. When I first confronted this heartbreaking, sinking feeling; the moaning; the grabbing for every morsel of food; the constant death, I accepted it with a silent scream—accepted it because there was absolutely nothing I could do about it.

Eventually I allowed myself to retreat from reality and dream or fantasize. When the cries of the wounded filled the barracks, when people were dying from pain and hunger, I would dream that I was back home with my parents, taking a bath and sleeping in a clean bed, eating freshly baked bread with butter. I missed my mother and father with a passion. I learned to think about them less and less so that I would not feel the pain of longing. My sister and I would fall asleep by recalling many pleasant memories of our home. We both consoled each other, and we gave each other strength and great moral support. We also told many funny stories and joked. It kept us sane.

Zellenappel, roll call, took place at six o'clock in the morning. We learned to stand at strict attention in spite of the bitter cold. We would stand for hours as a punishment if someone did something that displeased one of the guards. Then came our "breakfast" of diluted, bitter-tasting coffee and bread, sometimes with margarine. A screaming Aufseherin, a female warden, shouted the rules and regulations. If your hand wandered to your pocket during these tirades on bitter cold mornings, you would soon find that it was better to be cold than to have a rubber baton across your back. We were then marched a few kilometers to work outside the camp, heavily guarded by soldiers and dogs. I really could never understand the reason for this heavy guard. There was no possibility of escape, not with our numbers tattooed so visibly.

We were assigned to do heavy manual work, carrying heavy stones and building roads somewhere around Auschwitz, with a half-hour rest period. This routine continued for a number of months, although it seemed like years. Upon return from work each day, we were greeted by Tauber, then in charge of our camp, and either Dr. Mengele or Dr. Klein. Selections for the gas chambers would always be held. With the slight movement of his thumb and a faint smile on his face, life or death would be ordained. He would then say softly to the victim that she had lived long enough, and it was now time to go. Before returning to camp, we were forced to jump across a ditch about five feet wide. Those who made it were lucky and could survive to repeat this ordeal another day. Those who didn't would go to Block 25—the Death Block. The victim's number was written down as the inmate would try to get out from the ditch. That evening and night the gas chambers would roar with ferocity.

When the rest of us would return to the barracks, we greeted each other like long lost relatives. One would always find a faint smile or embrace. Most of the selections took place between January 1943 and June 1944. The majority of the millions who died in Auschwitz were consumed in that period. It became normal to walk out in the early morning roll call and see hundreds of emaciated bodies, still warm, piled up in front of the barracks. How did I stand it? One decided early on whether to go mad and commit suicide by approaching the all-surrounding, very high voltage electric fence, whose force would suck a person in if he came within five feet of it. Or one could accept the brutal fact that fate had singled one out among millions of Jewish victims to bear the burden of man's inhumanity to man. It became a sort of game to live through each day. I was grateful for each day, although there were many when I very much wanted to die.

Reality was so harsh that fantasy was a very necessary part of my existence. My will to live must have been very strong. Deep down I really didn't think I would ever see the outside world again. At that time, to survive Auschwitz was a dream. There was some kind of pattern—if you made it the first few days, you made it for the week. Then if a few weeks passed and you escaped selection, you could make it for a month. And it continued so on. Rays of hope would flicker occasionally, and as time went on, you almost dared to imagine a sane future. We had no contact with the outside world, so news of the war was simply not available to us. Every now and then, a rumor would spread that the Russian army was advancing, but we felt that the Germans in charge of Auschwitz would never allow us to leave the camp alive.

During our time in the ghetto and in Auschwitz, Sala was my anchor and protector. She kept my morale up and would not let me become pessimistic; she encouraged me in every way to keep thinking positive thoughts in spite of the horrors and hardships around us. She was strong in body and spirit. We would huddle together on the narrow triple-decker bunk we shared with three other women. She would talk to me about our home and dreaming of eating fresh bread and butter. We knew that our parents had been brought here five months earlier and were no longer alive. Even until this day, I cannot fathom how they died. I know of course, but I cannot bear to face that reality...

One particular memory has haunted me for years. On a freezing February morning shortly after our arrival, Sala and I were standing in line during a Zellenappel to receive our daily sustenance. On that morning, in addition to the stale slice of bread, we were also given a thin slice of salami and a slice of cheese. I knew that from childhood, my sister did not like dairy food. She turned to me gently and asked if I would exchange my slice of salami for her slice of cheese. I said no; I had really wanted to eat the slice of salami. I did not trade our food and grant her small request. Even now I still think about that little incident with great pain for having been so selfish. I would have given her my life…

On Friday, April 8th 1943, after three months in Auschwitz, my sister became very sick. Although I was younger and frequently ill as a child, Sala had very rarely been sick. I pleaded with her to get up and try to go with her assigned work commando in spite of the severe pains in her legs. She could hardly stand. I knew that remaining even one day sick in camp would mean certain death. Selections were held during the day and numbers of the sick inmates were written on that fateful pad. The infirm were removed shortly thereafter. I reluctantly brought her to Block 25, supposedly the hospital from which very few ever returned.

On Sunday, I went to see her again and found her delirious with fever, pleading that she had to go out and buy me a birthday present. Sala's illness was probably typhoid. On that Sunday, April 10th 1943, the day before my 14th birthday, Sala died as I held her in my arms. My strong, beautiful, athletic, and healthy sister expired after three months in hell. She was only nineteen.

I was devastated and cried very bitterly that day, and then I couldn't cry for many years. I became very unfeeling, very strong inside. The luxury of self-pity was not possible. Allowing depression to develop inside a concentration camp meant unavoidable self-destruction. If the mind was still functioning, it could counteract intolerable circumstances. I realized at that

Martha

moment that I was totally alone in the world. My sister's body was placed among the corpses I had seen every morning in front of the barracks. She joined these wretched human beings with a faint smile.

A woman watching my sister's death came toward me and addressed me in German that I did not understand too well. She told me that if she had a child, a little girl, she would want her to look like me. "I know that you are alone now. I am much older than you. Let me take care of you," she said. And she did.

Her name was Martha. She was a nurse before the war and had come to Auschwitz a few months before from Zilina in Slovakia. We communicated in her broken Polish. Eventually I learned German from her. Sala was my first angel; Martha was my second angel. I was destined on four different occasions to go to the gas chambers, my number having been written down, and on each occasion, a miracle occurred which reprieved me. Martha was able to talk and persuade the doctor with whom she worked to remove my number from his pad. During a long illness, I was hidden by the non-Jewish inmates in the Aryan hospital. Martha would steal life-giving medicines and, with the help of the other inmates, would feed me intravenously. I couldn't eat for a long time.

Eventually I was transferred to Lager (Compound) C. The warden in charge was the beautiful, cruel, twenty-year-old Irma Grese. I was assigned to be a Lauferin, a messenger. This meant that I did not have to work outside, but I delivered messages within the camp for the guards or officers. I was totally petrified of Grese who I quickly learned was a lesbian. She was never without a great German shepherd. She once told me that I reminded her of her sister, and perhaps because of that, she took a liking to me. I was glad that I was so underdeveloped because instead of making love to me, I stood guard at the barracks while she made love to the more beautiful Jewish girls. I was allowed to clean her uniform and clean her boots, and for that I would get extra rations from her private food supply. Irma Grese was convicted and executed at the Nuremberg trials.

For a number of months, I also worked in Brzezinka, where the crematoria were, sorting the clothing of the gassed victims. I accepted it, once again, simply because there was no alternative.

One became numb and learned to accept the hell of Auschwitz almost as a matter of fact. Was there really another world out there? Could the same sun shine on such misery and also on free people? It was so difficult to believe....

Two years after liberation, in August 1947, I wrote an article for *The Jewish Monthly* of London summarizing one day in Auschwitz ....

> It is half past three in the morning. It is dark; the stars dot the sky; and the moon, still a bit sleepy, casts its shadows on the sorry sight of our barracks at Auschwitz.
>
> Their inmates are submerged in the hard slumber of the weary and exhausted. No covers, no mattresses, in spite of the penetrating cold, their sleep is nonetheless deep. The frost displays its frolicsome pranks on the windowpanes, and the thin snow playfully scatters flakes.
>
> The silence is torn asunder by a sigh. Oh, how cold it is! A mournful cry of a childish voice is heard: "God, have mercy! My mother is dying!" This is how I pass the terrible nights, where our mothers, sisters, and fathers are dying by the hundreds and thousands.
>
> Nearly frozen, I am stretched out on my hard wooden shelf. What will tomorrow bring? Will I be lucky enough to spend another night on the narrow and dirty shelf? My mind keeps on working. What shall I do? Can I continue to live this way?
>
> Surely, a selection will take place tomorrow. I am still so young, and yet I have no right to live. There are few if any children in the camp. God,

if they knew that I am only fourteen years old!

Penetrating whistles cut short my thoughts. So the night has passed. I am sobering up. Again begins the sad, monotonous camp day. The hoarse voices of the night guards are bellowing: "Aufstehen! Zellenappel."

I rise quickly, as if driven mad, in order to get myself ready for the line-up. There is no thought of washing where people are dying of thirst. Who can afford to wash? Hurriedly I eat my meager breakfast, a dry crust of bread and a drop of cold, bitter coffee. Shall I finish the little piece of bread now? There is a long day of hard work ahead. What will I eat at the end of the day? The chase begins.

We are driven out of the barracks. We line up in columns of five for the roll call. I would have loved to remain in the barracks just once. I can't stand it any longer. The frost pinches my cheeks mercilessly, and my feet are just beginning to refuse obedience. But I know that should I remain in the barracks but once, my life will come to an end. No, I want to live! I will fight for my life. Life is not a plaything, although I know little of it because I have not managed to learn enough about it during my fourteen years in the world. And I give myself some encouragement.

Again, the whistle interrupts my thoughts, and the horrible voice of the female supervisor shrieks: "Arbeitsformierung! Zur Arbeit, faule Bande! [Line up for work! To work, you filthy lot!]" Beatings resound. More than one stick is broken on human shoulders, and in spite of my wishes I must again march for the exhausting work.

The silky white snow scatters itself about. Around us is a beautiful winter scene. but, my soul does not feel this beauty. My eyes can barely see it.

There is nothing but bitterness and sorrow in my heart. I lean over my spade and try energetically to pick at the frozen soil. Now and then the supervisor begins to drive us, and I feel a terrible pain of the whip striking me for no reason. A few steps from me, a girl is passing out from the cold, hunger, and thirst. Clandestinely, I swallow my tears. I do not want to cry. I do not want to show a sign of my suffering. I am not even allowed to go over to her. I keep thinking about the "lunch" recess. Hunger gnaws at me and I feel that my knees are about to give way. Finally, the midday whistle is heard. We stand in line and I impatiently wait my turn for a gulp of cold cabbage soup.

The recess passes quickly. The hard work begins again. The hours are unending. It is only one o'clock. Sad thoughts depress me. I think of the evening check-off and am terribly frightened. There surely will be a selection. Oh God, do not leave me! I want to survive all this to bear witness for the mad injustice, for the deaths of my dearest and sweetest mother, loving father, and beloved sister. Somehow, I am able to emerge into my inner world of fantasy.

Finally, the workday is over, and we are being lined up to return to the camp. We are shifted about, beaten and endlessly counted. They keep checking if anyone is missing. They must account for each inmate on the entrance to the camp gate. This is the favorite pastime for the cruel guards. With the help of the vicious German Shepherds, the power they hold over us has gone to their heads. They feel very important. We slowly begin to walk.

It is far from the camp, and the road is muddy and slippery. After a long and exhausting march, we see afar the Blockfuehrer's quarters. These are always the decisive minutes. We approach the camp and are greeted by Tauber's horrible voice: "What kind of group is this? Is this mostly a Jewish group?" Without much ado, he begins to sort us out. His face is aflame with joy, the face of a man who holds power over his "herd". He will soon have merchandise for the crematoria. That is where those who don't make the grade, according to him, wind up. We all know that. We are made to jump over a ditch to check if we are still physically capable of returning to work the next day. "Come on, come on, schnel," he shouts. "You can do it."

I am unable to describe what went on in my heart. I do not know how I remained alive. The fear, the fright that comes before death! What a terrible feeling when a person knows that he is going to his doom. It makes little difference if one is young or old, according to Tauber: everyone is fit for death if you are Jewish. The furnace will welcome all. About 100 of us in this group started out, and only 60 returned to camp. This is how they are finishing off our lives. Those who did not wind up in the crematoria when they were first transported here, sooner or later, go there anyway.

Finally, we have reached our Block. I look around; my closest friend is no longer with us. Immersed in sad thoughts, I hear the lineup whistle. I no longer cry. My heart must be harder than stone. The block leader counts us off. Her loud count seems to be that of an automaton. Generally, my entire life appears automatic. I do not feel anything except hunger and cold. All would appear to be a cruel cream, were it not for the piercing "Achtung" torn out of the block leader's jaws. Although we are all hardly able to stand, we try to remain in formation without faltering. The check-off seems endless.

Night had fallen long ago. Life appears like a will o' the wisp without an end. We are admitted to the block. It is pitch dark. Everyone pushes ahead. Everyone wants to be first, for fear that there may not be enough food for all, that she may not get a blanket. But alas, not all of us are in their customary places. Half have been taken to Block 25, the Death Block.

It is dark and cold. There are crying sights of wounded hearts. There is light coming from the chimneys, it burns like fireworks. Everyone misses someone. No one has a friendly word.

GOD, IF YOU EXIST, SOS!

Chapter 3

Lucien

In preparation for one of the occasional talks I gave, I looked through my papers and came across a folder marked "Lucien". Years had passed since I last opened it. Inside was a paper that had become increasingly yellowed with age. It was a poem written in German. Next to it was a photograph depicting a handsome young man. Lucien, I thought, how long ago it was and how vividly I remember that unusual episode in my life. The memory of Lucien is a treasure I cherish. He touched me deeply and made an indelible impression on me. I began to read to myself, aloud, and the poem conjured up memories that lay just beneath the surface. The words jumped out of the page. "In remembrance of a tragic, and yet so enchantingly beautiful and sad time…" I had known him only three months of my life, but I will always remember him. The story unfolded before my eyes and suddenly emerged to life…

It was still dark when I awoke from a dreamy, restless sleep in April 1945 at a camp called Retzow-am-Rechlin. Without opening my eyes, I allowed my thoughts to drift carelessly to the lovely park where I played as a child. The memories appeared misty and so far away. It all seemed like eons ago, somewhere in another life, on another planet. The gentle autumn wind was blowing my hair as I was chasing a ball, stepping over the freshly fallen leaves, and picking up the shiny round fruits of the chestnut trees that covered the ground. I used to collect different multi-colored leaves and chestnuts as a hobby, and every autumn I would spend pleasant hours arranging them neatly according to size and color.

My mother would lovingly watch my innocent play and carefree fun, and she would occasionally direct my attention to an unusual birch leaf while sitting on a wooden bench reading a book. I would wander off and then hear the echo of mother's mellow voice coming across the pond calling for me not to stray too far away. I was back home in Grodno, riding horseback with my father on his chestnut-colored steed in the woods...listening to my mother sing while she prepared our dinner...hearing my sister play the guitar... These were carefree days filled with love and security. All these memories were now only distant recollections of times past, embedded deeply in my mind in clouds of nostalgic, distant thoughts.

Unwillingly, I finally opened my eyes, and the familiar surroundings jolted me back to reality. Turning lazily to one side, I peeked through the opening of the wooden wall next to my bunk. The faint glow of the early morning sun cast its shadow on the barren earth.

Even before the shrill sound of the siren indicating the beginning of another meaningless and monotonous day, I permitted myself the luxury of a few moments of solitude before the rush of the inevitable morning roll call.

Hastily putting on my striped dress and holding my wooden shoes in my hands so as not to rouse the other inmates, I quietly snuck out of the barracks. I stood momentarily undisturbed, breathing the fresh air in the solitude of the early spring morning. A bird chirped away securely perched on the branch of a budding tree, not knowing that happy sounds were totally alien to the wary inhabitants below in this forsaken prison camp. I wish I could have turned into a bird and flown away! Was there still another world somewhere to fly to?

For a brief moment, I let my thoughts turn to dreams of freedom. For the past 45 months—almost four years—I had become conditioned to the inevitable predicament of the sinister claws of death. I never thought I would see freedom, but how and when the end would come, none of us knew. We carried our death certificates on our forearms from which only the date was missing. From Ghetto, Auschwitz, and Ravensbruck, and now to Retzow-am-Rechlin, our transport arrived here from Ravensbruck in early February when the ground was heavily covered with snow. But where was the next stop? Rumors started to circulate that the war was coming to an end, and I harbored unrealistic thoughts that maybe, maybe I would really survive this hell... It was a lovely fantasy that kept my spirits up.

The morning sun was beginning to cast its golden rays around me, creating dark and fascinating shadows. In this momentary solitude, the gentle breeze caressed my face and hair that had grown back to a golden blond after the total shaving at Auschwitz. This morning I thought of life. I wanted to live very much. I was approaching my sixteenth birthday, and somewhere deep inside, I was beginning to feel the wonder of nature within me. Underdeveloped and deprived, nature nevertheless played havoc with me, letting me know that I was growing into a woman.

The shrill sound of the siren announcing the Zellenappell cut through the air jolting me back to reality. We learned to stand in strict attention, sometimes for hours in freezing weather, depending on the whim of the *Aufseherin*. After the countdown, we were given "breakfast" consisting of a slice of stale black bread, diluted coffee, and a slab of sour-tasting margarine. The work *Kommandos* would form amidst screaming guards and huge, growling German Shepherd dogs. After the inspection, we would automatically line up for work duty and march off to our assigned destination. Another heavy-laden day would begin.

I was brought to Retzow by heavy army trucks after two years of Auschwitz and three weeks in Ravensbruck. Retzow was located about 90 kilometers from Berlin, somewhere deep in the heart of the Third Reich. The camp was adjacent to a munitions factory where V-2 bombers were being manufactured. I later learned that they had devastated London. The majority of inmates were put to work at the factory. Others were assigned to a forest kommando where they chopped down trees and cut them into pieces of wood to aid the war production.

When we finally landed in Retzow and were initially processed, I was asked what kind of work I did in Auschwitz. I told them I was a Lauferin, a messenger for the officers and guards in the main Blockfuehrerstube. "Good," said the stocky and mean looking officer, "we need an experienced Lauferin here. Put this on your left sleeve and wear it all the time." He gave me a broad bandanna with heavily gothic lettering imprinted with the word *Lauferin*. I was instructed to stand guard inside the camp gates and deliver messages for the guards and officers from the central headquarters located just outside the camp compounds. At all times, a sentry armed with a rifle was watching the prisoners from a tall guard-post structure towering above the barracks.

When the work Kommandos left the campgrounds escorted by heavily armed guards and leashed dogs, the camp assumed the markings of a "normal day". I would dutifully position myself at the inside gates, ready and awaiting the commands of my captors.

On that morning, perhaps it was the onset and sweet smell of spring, the awakening of nature, that made me feel nostalgic and put me into a dream-like mood that gave way to hope, momentarily dispelling the deep scars of years of suffering. I let my thoughts drift back again to my world of fantasy, relieving my tormented soul. Retzow was carved out from a forest, and there were still many trees surrounding the campgrounds. Little wild flowers kept emerging everywhere, ignoring the cruelty of man. Even the barbed wire could not diminish nature's wonders.

I looked up at the sky. It was so blue and clear that it looked transparent. I wondered if free people outside the camps in other parts of the world were looking at the same sky. Did anyone know what was going on in my world?

I was overwhelmed with a desire to run to the woods, uninhibited: to touch someone that belonged to me; to embrace; to hug; to feel life free of barbed wire and endless uncertainty and torment. I longed to indulge in all the activities I used to take for granted in the short spell of my early childhood: to eat freshly baked bread with butter, delivered to our home fresh from the farms; to take a warm bath; to indulge in carefree play with my friends, all of whom had since been killed. I missed the sounds of music, which were so much a part of my days at home. Everything about my childhood became a precious dream, and I was clinging to those memories with a stubborn tenacity. The beasts had taken away everything else; memories they couldn't take away from me. With all this day dreaming, I thought: *Oh well, spring is having a strong effect on me. It will pass. Keep dreaming*, I consoled myself, *that's all that is left.* Freedom appeared to be so near and yet so hopelessly far, if ever...

I was softly humming a song my mother sang to me many years ago, and suddenly I became aware that I was being deliberately watched by the guard. He had been in the camp for the past two months, but we had never exchanged words, except when he gave me a specific order. For the past few weeks, he was assigned to guard duty. He leaned over, resting his rifle over the railing. He was smiling at me! In the last forty-five months, I learned to sense the moods and behavior of the peculiar breed of concentration camp guards. I was sure they were chosen for their sadistic predisposition. Most were terribly cruel and thoroughly enjoyed inflicting great pain on their victims.

But this guard betrayed no sarcasm. His friendly behavior was a sign I did not understand. I had seen him when he accompanied the forest kommando during their daily formation, and he typically assumed the abrasive tone of voice expected of concentration camp guards. His fellow comrades nicknamed him Booby, probably because he looked so innocent and young. This morning his behavior did not reveal what I was generally accustomed to. This guard acted differently. He smiled at me, and without saying anything, he began to sing a German song unfamiliar to me, *"Zwein Himmel Blaue Augen"* (Two Sky-Blue Eyes).

The word "Achtung" cut through the air with a piercing sound. The young guard drew to attention, with his rifle firmly on his shoulder and gave the customary salute, "Heil Hitler!" I stood motionless as the Kommandant was entering the gates for his morning inspection. Achtung had become the most familiar word in my vocabulary, and yet I always froze whenever I heard it.

The Kommandant, accompanied by three officers of his staff, was about to inspect his domain. He threw an icy glance in my direction and, with a goosestep precision, proceeded to enter the campgrounds. He was a short, broad-shouldered, stocky man, and he was immaculately groomed. Many shiny medals decorated his spotless uniform. When he gave me orders, his eyes would narrow expressing a look of intense concentration. His voice had a staccato-like quality, the typical guttural tones of a German officer. He spoke very rapidly, as though the day was not long enough for him to accomplish all he wanted. I was very frightened of him.

The inspection would last about an hour every morning. He stopped briefly at the gate, occasionally giving me a specific instruction, and then he left the campgrounds as rapidly as he entered. The gate would close; his chauffeur standing at attention opened the car door; the guard repeated "Heil Hitler"; and within minutes, the car drove away. I would start breathing again. God, how many times did the Kommandant's inspection mean immediate liquidation of the sick, never to be seen again? In this camp, there were no crematoria. People just died from illness, starvation, and exhaustion.

With the daily inspection ritual over, I took a deep breath of relief and retrieved back to my own little private world. I looked up at Booby. He no longer stood at attention. He seemed relaxed and smiled at me again. Perhaps he guessed my thoughts and my fears. Perhaps he too wished to be out of his uniform and back with his family. He seemed so young. I wondered where he came from, what compelled him to join the ranks of the German army. Was his father a Nazi? Was he a dedicated member of the Hitler Youth, obeying his Fatherland

and proud of it? How many dead prisoners does he carry on his conscience?

I suddenly heard my name: "Fraulein Nelli"... Oh yes, there was no mistake about it. He called my name. Fraulein Nelli? Who ever heard a guard speaking that way to an inmate! How did he know my name? We were generally known by numbers, not names. We were usually barked at, not spoken to, and we were certainly not addressed with the polite appellation "Miss" as a normal person would be. I looked up at the post.

"Ja," I answered in puzzlement. By this time I had acquired a solid knowledge of German and spoke it fluently.

"Don't look so shocked. I didn't mean to startle you." He realized how surprised I was and reassured me that he only wanted to talk to me.

"Yes, what would you like me to do?" I answered quietly and lifted my eyes in his direction.

"Please, Fraulein Nelli, don't make it obvious that we are speaking. You know of course that we are not allowed to speak to inmates when on duty, unless we give official orders." Oh yes, I knew! I was well acquainted with camp rules! What did he want?

I looked to see if other guards were in the vicinity, but no one was there. The conversation was strange. Actually it was he who was speaking and I who was listening. He spoke softly and rapidly, as if he had stored up everything for this moment. His voice betrayed a sense of strange excitement and an unmistakable anxiety. He looked very earnest.

Almost apologetically he asked, "What are you doing in this camp? I mean, how did you get here and why? I have been watching you ever since I was assigned to Retzow. You are so young and lovely, you can't be more than fourteen years old!"

I was sure there was a catch somewhere. No German guard asked such inane questions. I thought he had a weird sense of humor, entertaining himself at my expense. What am I doing here? Ha! Where had he been the last four years? I answered politely and stiffly, not looking at him. "I am Jewish. I was brought here from Auschwitz and Ravensbruck. As far as I know, I am the only member of my family still alive. I will be sixteen soon."

He must have realized from the expression on my face that I was puzzled, but he continued anyway. "Fraulein Nelli, listen to me, please. My name is Lucien. I am not German. I am from Luxembourg, the part that borders the western half of Germany. I am nineteen, and until last year, I was enrolled in the University as a medical student. I was drafted into the German army a year ago, and I had no knowledge what was going on here. I learned about the atrocities and the madness only recently. I was forced to join the army. I had no choice. I was sent here as a relief guard. I had no idea what terrible things are being done to the Jews. I learned the horror tales from the accounts of the seasoned, older guards. I couldn't believe how casually they talk about tortures. I dream about the horrors at night. Back home, we knew the plight of the Jews but had no idea what was really going on. You see, I didn't think you were Jewish, and that's why I asked you why you are here."

I listened in utter disbelief. I was stunned. He sounded totally convincing, and I believed he was telling the truth. Why else would he say such things and unburden his feelings? I was not quite sixteen and had already lived many lives. I was a seasoned concentration camp inmate. I knew life as a prisoner, but very little of the "other world" outside my sheltered childhood. Could it be that he knew little about the atrocities of war and Hitler's master plan to annihilate the Jewish population of Europe? Didn't people in the free world know what was going on here?

His voice sounded so genuine, so full of emotion, so soft and pleading. I looked at him again. He was well built; his blond hair showed through his military cap with the Nazi emblem. He had a handsomely childish face, with full lips and soft blue eyes. He seemed so tall standing there.

Lucien suddenly drew to full attention again and uttered "Achtung". A car was pulling up, and two officers entered the Blockfuehrerstube. Officers from the munitions plant frequently paid visits to the camp.

The brief conversation with Lucien left me strangely puzzled. Could it be that even those wearing a German uniform can feel compassion and care for what happens to an inmate? *How odd*, I thought. I simply was not prepared for anyone wearing that uniform to speak to me in a civilized manner, ask personal questions, or care about me as a human being.

Shortly after the visit from the officers, Lucien was relieved by another guard. At the end of the day when the work Kommandos came back, I joined them for our meager evening nourishment. I ran to the barracks and my little space in the bunk I shared with three other girls. There were only women here, about 1500. I didn't know where they sent the men. I was overcome with strange feelings. What Lucien had said to me and the manner in which he had said it all stuck in my mind. I was touched by his obvious feelings of sincerity. What compelled him to talk to me? I didn't understand. Concentration camp guards were known to be inhumane, but this guard was different.

During the following weeks, Lucien and I spoke often. He would initiate the conversation during my duties at the gate, or he would find me in the camp compounds. He would frequently ask me about my life: where I was from, what my family was like. He wanted to know about my hardships at Auschwitz. He would frequently say, "Tell me more about yourself and your family life, what you liked most about school." He brought an eerie sense of normalcy into our conversation.

"Tell me something about yourself," I would ask of him. I sensed great uneasiness in him.

"I want to tell you so many things about my life too," he would answer. "I had a comfortable upbringing, a loving family, just like you. I was enrolled at the University to study medicine. Well, now I am here and learning of the horrible atrocities of the war. You see, we are really both victims in a sense, although I don't mean to compare myself to your incredible suffering. I am supposed to be your enemy, but please believe me, I am not. Don't ever stop dreaming and hoping. Your dreams may come true. You have so much to live for."

Lucien wanted to be my friend. But how could that be? His caring for me and his gentle demeanor made me feel that he was probably right, that we both were victims of Hitler's madness, on the opposite poles of the spectrum. I sensed feelings of great sadness in him and, at the same time, a genuine concern for me. I became strangely drawn to him and experienced a sense of confusion. I didn't believe that the word "humanity" still existed outside the dictionary, and yet here was someone who touched me, a German guard! No wonder I was confused.

In moments of dreaming I dared to hope that maybe some day I may be free and experience the wonders of love. Then ominous thoughts would overshadow any glimmer of hope for survival. I was sure they would never let us go to bear witness to their atrocities. I didn't know that the end of the war was near and that I would be one of the few lucky ones to survive.

A few days later while I was eating in the camp kitchen (because I worked inside the camp, I was given permission to eat there), I suddenly saw Lucien enter. I overheard him speaking to the SS Matron in charge. He must have asked her for something. She gave him a polite smile and left the kitchen. For the first time I found myself alone with him. He walked with a steady pace to the small table at the end of the kitchen where I was sitting.

Our eyes met. His eyes were the most intense and blue in color I have ever seen. I felt strangely uncomfortable and a bit frightened. I sensed that he too felt uneasy. He stood a few feet away from me and glanced to see whether anyone was near us. Satisfied that no one was watching he came closer to my bench while I continued to eat, secretly glancing at him. He hesitated at first and then spoke softly. "I have been assigned to guard the forest Kommando. I'll probably be with them for a few weeks, and I want you to get transferred to that unit. I must speak to you away from this place and what I have to say cannot be said here. I know the Kommandant likes you, and if you ask for his permission, he will probably let you go. I have something very important to tell you. Do it quickly."

We heard the footsteps of the Matron approaching, and he quickly walked away from me. The Matron handed him a package wrapped in brown paper. She smiled at him, and they exchanged a few words of pleasantries. He thanked her and quickly walked out. He left me feeling puzzled. I could not imagine what it was he wanted to tell me with such great urgency.

The following morning after the Kommandant's routine inspection, I asked permission to speak to him. He threw a cold glance at me and bluntly said, "Come with me." I followed him to the Blockfuehrerstube. "What do you want, Lauferin?" I couldn't believe where I mustered up my courage. A feeling of great fear engulfed me. This stern looking man was very intimidating. I reasoned with myself that after all, I did see him every day, and he knows who I am.

With great trepidation, I began, "Herr Kommandant, I came to ask for permission to be transferred to the forest Kommando. I have never worked outside the campgrounds. The other Lauferin has already rotated; I suppose it soon will be my turn. Please forgive my boldness." I tried very hard not to tremble, but I felt my knees weakening under me. It was unusual for an inmate ever to request anything, particularly from a Kommandant, but this was a different kind of camp, smaller than most and a bit more relaxed in discipline. There were no death selections. It was known as a work camp rather than an extermination camp.

The Kommandant eyed me carefully, walked slowly and deliberately over to me, almost with a sense of amusement, and mockingly said, "So you would like to go into the world and work in the forest, would you? Well, you look strong enough to chop trees and carry heavy logs. Hard work will do you good. Yes, you go with them. Permission granted." Arrogantly, as though talking to himself in amusement, he repeated, "You want to leave the camp grounds, do you? Now go". That was that. I thanked him politely and ran out of the Blockfuehrerstube. I was shaking all over and my heart was pounding so rapidly I thought it would jump out of my body.

The following morning I joined the forest Kommando. As I marched with the women, one said, "Welcome to slavery, and keep up your strength, little one." The inmates were generally divided into groups of 200, and each group was accompanied by eight heavily armed guards—as though any of us could ever think of escaping. The grotesque Auschwitz tattoo, number 31386, left me branded for life. Here I was known as number 106487. There could never be an escape, even here. Lucien was one of the guards in my group and tacitly acknowledged my presence when our eyes met.

We marched about two miles and finally reached a heavily wooded area. We were given instructions, administered with loud, abrasive tones. The guards never talked to us. They always shouted. But I was more afraid of the ferocious-looking German Shepherd dogs. It brought terrible memories of Auschwitz when these dogs were unleashed at a prisoner at the whim of a guard for the slightest infraction; they could mutilate a prisoner in minutes.

I was assigned to chop and carry the logs to a designated area in a clearing of the forest. Later, trucks would pick up the wood and use it in some aspect for war production. Lucien now assumed the role of tough guy. He walked to my assigned post and openly started to criticize my ineptitude, shouting at me. He succeeded in the role of the master over his prisoners, but the part somehow didn't fit him. I detected an artificial tone in his voice. As time passed, my arms became terribly tired from the heavy manual labor. In Auschwitz, I carried stones. Here I carry wood. I began to wonder whether an opportunity would arise for us to talk. The guards were scattered around, smoking cigarettes and talking among themselves while keeping a close watch over us.

Lucien tapped me on my shoulder and loudly ordered me to follow him to work in another area of the forest. I obeyed like a trained dog and walked away with him. Everyone could hear him shouting at me. I knew what he was doing. I was relieved that he finally found the right moment to drag me away. We found ourselves a bit further away from the others in a more isolated part of the forest. Except for sounds of voices and falling logs, there was on one in the immediate vicinity.

His voice now changed to the mellow tone I heard when he first spoke to me. "Nelli, I want to tell you how glad I am that you managed to be transferred here. I know this is very hard work, but I want to talk to you about a matter of vital importance. So please listen carefully and say nothing. You realize of course that I had to make a scene there for the benefit of the others, or they may have suspected something. I could be punished as severely as you. I don't want the other guards to suspect anything. I don't trust them."

He continued soberly in a whisper. "Listen, the war is coming to an end; we all know that. We are surrounded on all sides by the Russians, the Americans, and the British. The top hierarchy is getting very nervous because they know the end is near. We get new reports of the devastation of the German armies every day. It can't last much longer. Panic is bound to follow, particularly regarding the fate of concentration camp survivors. At the moment, everything is still the same, but that will change. No new orders about the prisoners have come in, but the word is floating around that the inmates of this camp may be marked for liquidation, so that no hard evidence is found. There is no question that the Germans are kaput. Before they have a chance to take you away from here, I must help you."

He looked at me with a steady gaze. I listened with fear and trepidation to his monologue while he encouraged me to keep on working. The whole episode was incongruous. I couldn't believe what I was hearing. I put my hand to my mouth in astonishment to protect myself from screaming out. How unreal for a Jewish girl in a Nazi camp standing in the woods with a soldier wearing a German uniform, armed with a gun and a dog, who wants to help her escape! I was looking at his uniform, looking at his eyes, listening to his words, but being reminded by the reality of what he represented. Trust him? I must be dreaming, it couldn't be real, but I listened attentively as he continued.

"Nelli," he said tenderly, "I want to help you in any way I can. Listen carefully. Since I was transferred here, I have known a German woman who lives near the village on a small farm a few kilometers away. I have arranged with her to let you hide in her cellar until the war is over. She promised to give me civilian clothes for you. When the time is right, I will take you there. Trust me. When the evacuation orders come, there will be much confusion. Nobody will really care much any more. It will be the perfect opportunity to sneak you out of here. There is no need to give you the details of my plan at this time. What is important is that I get you out of here soon, or it may be too late. She lost her husband and two sons herself and she feels very bitter about the war. She knows about this camp and promised to help me. Now, forget what I have told you, and don't breathe a word to anyone in the camp about this or we will both hang."

I felt numb all over. Did I really understand what he was saying to me? Go into hiding? Survive the war with the help of a German soldier? Someone actually cares what happens to me? "Why do you want to take such a risk to help me?" I asked quietly. "Why do I deserve your concern for me?" Booby looked at me and his eyes suddenly swelled up. A strange feeling overwhelmed me, a feeling I had not experienced before.

"Liebchen, you are naive not to have noticed how I feel about you. You are so lovely, so young and innocent in spite of the hardships you endured these awful years. Haven't you guessed that I love you? Don't you understand? I love you, and I don't want you to die. I never dreamt that anyone could stir me to such deep and tender emotion. The love I feel for you is more that I can express at this moment. I want to hold you and kiss you and protect you. I know that time will come. The only thing I can do now is to make sure that you are safe. I must help you." Lucien kept repeating, "I must help you. I want you to live" over and over as though he wanted to reassure himself that he could really make it happen. I looked at him, bewildered by what had just transpired. He came closer and stretched out his hand to mine. He held it tenderly. "Look at the ugly blisters on your hands. Don't worry, little one. They will go away. Don't lose hope and have faith in the future."

Silence fell. I sensed his desire to take me in his arms and kiss me. He continued to hold my hands and kissed them gently, He finally said, "You better get back with the others." Lucien had awakened feelings in me I did not know existed.

The entire episode seemed unreal. Escape, hiding, love, a future? These were totally alien thoughts from a totally alien world. I finally broke the silence by thanking him and saying how touched I was by his sentiments. I mumbled that what he proposed was probably unrealistic. I knew what they did to people who even mildly entertained the thought of escape. I remembered vividly a beautiful Polish Jewish inmate hanging from the gallows in Auschwitz after being severely tortured when she was caught trying to escape. Things were different here, but the penalty, I was sure, was the same.

In April of 1945, I had little choice. We were probably going to be killed anyway, so I agreed. Lucien assured me that he had planned this for the past few weeks, and he took great care to make sure everything would go smoothly. The woman on the farm, he assured me, promised to hide me. He did not elaborate how it would finally be accomplished. "I will tell you everything when all the arrangements are made. Lebewohl, my liebchen!" he said.

A few minutes later, I joined the rest of the commando. I was physically there, but my thoughts were miles away. There were still people in this world who care about others after all. But how unlikely the source! What a strange twist of fate!

I worked with the forest commando for two weeks and returned to my duties as Lauferin. Lucien and I continued to talk. He was also back at the guard post. He took every opportunity to seek me out whenever possible within the confines of the campgrounds. He would continue to assure me that the plan he proposed in the forest would work out. "I have spoken with my friend at the farm, and as soon as it is possible, I will smuggle you out of here." He gave me feelings of security and hope, and something more. I missed him if a day or two went by and I did not see him. I thought I was in love. It was a splendid little secret I harbored within me. I did not share my feelings with anyone else.

When we met, he would talk to me about our lives after the war, and my eyes would fill up with tears. "Why are you crying?" he would ask.

"Because you talk of freedom and sharing our lives together as though it will really happen. This is the first time in many years since I have cried, since the last time I held my dying sister in my arms in Auschwitz. You see, Lucien, these tears are now flowing out of tenderness rather than sorrow." I had allowed myself to feel something beyond grief and was unaccustomed to that emotion. "You have touched me very deeply. I hope we will always be friends if we survive this madness." He kept reassuring me that we would.

"I hope we will be more than friends," he said. "I know you have lost your entire family. I want to take you home to my family in Luxembourg. My family is very kind and will help to heal the wounds." I felt very strong emotions toward Lucien, far beyond the kindness he had shown me. I wanted him to protect me from the world. I wanted to be with him; I loved him. I began to dream childish dreams about Luxembourg, a country I knew nothing about.

At the end of April, we learned that orders were abruptly received that all the younger officers and guards were to be sent to the front within twenty-four hours. The air raids increased with a marked frequency. The munitions plant where most inmates worked, we were told, was severely damaged. I stood in front of the barracks, and with fascination, I watched the heavy cluster of red lights far up in the sky as the heavy bombers glided over the German skies. Yes, there was another world after all! The roar of exploding bombs made a wonderful sound. It was music to my ears. I was not frightened by the possibility of being killed by an American or Russian bomb. If I have to die, let me be killed that way than being shot somewhere in the woods. I stood outside my bunk, and a guard would yell at me to get inside. "Maybe it's not over yet. We just heard on the radio that President Roosevelt has died." America was a land million miles away, in another galaxy...

The following day as he was walking off his post, Lucien loudly and abruptly announced, "Lauferin, deliver my dinner tray to my office at the Kommandantur." It was not unusual for me to deliver dinner trays to the officers, but Lucien had never asked me to do so before. I was startled and elated at the same time because I was hoping that he would tell me that the time had come for him to smuggle me out of the camp. I kept thinking of nothing else as I stood guard for the rest of the afternoon. I knew something was going on. Officers were running around; cars were coming and going; and there seemed to be a general state of confusion.

I walked from the kitchen carrying the dinner tray and a guard opened the gate for me. I entered the Kommandantur with great trepidation, almost secretly, as though I anticipated something ominous. A state of confusion prevailed inside too. Officers were running in and out of their rooms as I walked into the main hall. Telephones were ringing all over. It seemed that nobody paid much attention to my being there.

A door opened and Lucien motioned for me to follow him. I entered behind him. He silently indicated to put the tray on his desk and gently closed the door. He was informally dressed and appeared pale and tense. I had always seen him in full uniform and never without a rifle. Tonight his jacket was unbuttoned revealing a clean white shirt and no tie. He nodded to me as though to acknowledge my presence. He seemed uneasy and vulnerable. My first impression was that perhaps someone had overheard our conversations or suspected something, and I felt frightened. I had never stayed behind closed doors with him. There was visible tension on his face, and I began to understand why he summoned me to his office on the pretext of bringing him dinner. It became obvious that my being there had little to do with my duties as Lauferin.

My being there was purely a private matter. I waited anxiously for him to speak. I was suddenly overcome with strange emotions. My body stiffened. It was not cold fear I was feeling. There was something else, something I did not understand. I had felt strange and unknown tenderness toward him since our meeting in the woods. How strange, I thought, finding myself alone in a room with him. I grew anxious for him to say something, but he just kept looking at me. Was he going to tell me tonight that his plan was in progress and he would sneak me out of the camp?

He played impatiently with his hands, and finally he reached into the jacket of his pocket and took out an envelope. Without looking at me, he spoke in a whisper. "I was informed last night that we are being transferred to the front. We are leaving tomorrow morning. The older guards will stay." A shiver went through my spine.

He looked up at me now and took a deep sigh. "I cannot help you get out of here, Nelli. There is no time." He paused momentarily. "I was awake all night thinking of you and have written a poem for you. When you read it you will understand my real feelings for you. You will also find a photograph of me in civilian clothes. Keep it with you always, and don't forget me. I only pray that you will get out of here alive."

I took the envelope from him with trembling hands. Lucien came closer; he took my hands and caressed them gently. He pushed up my left sleeve, looked at the grotesque tattoo on my left forearm, and kissed it. "You know, I have never been in love, and I don't even know how to tell you what I want to tell you. Words fail to express the love I hold for you. If we had met under normal circumstances, I would never let you go. You have done something quite extraordinary to me. I don't even understand it myself. All I know is that I hold the most tender feelings for you, and I long to hold you in my arms. I will always love you, and somehow I believe that we will meet again when all this

Lucien

is over. If I live, I will find you; we will be together. I will find you; I promise."

I felt my eyes filling up with tears again. It was the second time he brought out tears in me. *Strange*, I thought, *I cannot cry when I feel grief, but tears fill my eyes in moments of tenderness.*

I stood there holding on to the edge of the table when Lucien took me in his arms and held me very close. "Don't cry, liebchen," he said and kissed me firmly on my lips. He took my face in his hands, and his eyes looked at me with passion. He breathed heavily. "Dearest girl, do you know that it may be the last time I see you? Strange, is it not, that I, a soldier in Hitler's army, one of the many who have so wronged you, should be standing here asking you to forgive me for a crime I did not commit. But I am wearing the uniform of those who have done you so much harm."

His words kept pouring out in a whisper. "The last few months have been the most miserable and difficult in my life, and yet in a way, they were also the happiest because you have awakened deep love in me. He kissed me gently again. I remained locked in his arms, not understanding what was happening to me. I wanted to tell him that I loved him too, but I could not utter a word. I put the envelope safely in my pocket. I touched his face and wished him luck.

"Who knows?" I said quietly. "Maybe we will meet again soon. I will never forget you, Lebewohl, Lucien." I kissed him gently on his lips and squeezed his hands. I looked at him for the last time as he watched me walk out. The guard opened the gate for me and said, "What did you do there, clean the whole place?"

I ran to my barrack thinking that my heart would jump out of my body. I was clutching Booby's envelope. Oh, how I wanted to cry! How I wanted to share my thoughts with someone!

I was still deeply engrossed in my thoughts when evening gave way to night. I had never experienced the beauty and pain of love's longing. Inside me, nature stirred up pent-up emotions of a young woman. Yes, I felt love and joy, longing and pity, and great sadness. Would I ever experience the full measure of the culmination of nature's glorious gift, that of sharing my love with a man? I wanted more than ever to live. What cruel fate I thought, standing frustrated and confused on that beautiful April night! I was hoping for a glimpse of another world, a world that existed only in segments of my imagination when reality became too harsh, and I entered my private domain of fantasy. It was that fantasy that had kept me alive. Tonight fantasy gave way to reality. I felt a tender feeling of love toward Lucien.

The moon and stars were so bright that evening that I engaged myself in conversation with them, just the stars and I. I read and re-read Booby's poem by the light of the moon. He poured out the most glorious sentiments and love in an exquisite poetic form, and he told me to be brave. He would find me, and then we would be together; he would never let me go. Yes, I thought, that would be wonderful. I had never been kissed before, and I still felt his warm lips on mine. The feeling evoked such tender emotions in me. Oh Lucien, I miss you so.

I looked back at the Kommandantur and saw the light burning in his office. I was overwhelmed with great longing to be with him again. Only the millions of far away stars knew how I felt at that moment...

New guards replaced those who left, mostly Rumanians and Bulgarians. They were generally much older, and some were worse than the Germans. The days that followed brought great anxiety and uncertainty regarding our fate. The air raids continued at a greater pace. We were sure that we would be taken to the woods and shot. There was no question that the war was ending and with it, probably our lives as well. Lucien's letter and photograph was safely tucked away in my dress. It was my most important possession. Whenever I could, I read it and his words gave me courage to cling to hope. I missed seeing him very much.

A few days later we were rudely jolted from our sleep by the sound of a siren in the middle of the night. We were rounded up for a roll call, and we were told that we are being evacuated immediately. Panic erupted. We didn't believe them. We were sure we were going to be killed. I wished Lucien were still with me. He would have told me the truth. As we prepared to leave, I managed to take a few personal possessions including a small 1 x 2 inch pin neatly embroidered with number 106487, my number in this new camp, a birthday gift from a friend who worked as a seamstress for the officers. I pinned it on my dress, which was a bizarre thing to do. Did I want to die with an embroidered number pinned to my dress? The most important possession was in my dress pocket. I was clutching Lucien's poem and photograph.

Once again, as so many times before, we were driven out of the camp like obedient cattle and ordered to march—an evacuation, but where to? We marched hungry and exhausted night and day, stopping only for a little while every few hours. That rest was for the benefit of the guards. We didn't matter. The guards didn't really know what to do with us. It seemed like a journey without an end. Dear God, where was our destination? If they wanted to kill us, they would have done so in the woods. These were the questions on the minds of those of us who could still walk and still think. Would the liberators catch us in time?

The roar of the cannons were now coming closer. The guards were beginning to lose interest in their prisoners and worried more about themselves and the consequences they would face. Those wonderful sounds of bullets gave us encouragement and hope. If we could only survive this torturous march, perhaps freedom was not far away.

I kept thinking of Lucien's words: "Remain strong, my love. Persevere, and you will make it. I will find you." Poor wonderful Lucien, where was he? We continued to walk from sheer habit because there was no choice. Many did not make it. They fell by the wayside and were left there to die. Nobody could help them. There were no tears left to cry for them.

I couldn't stop thinking about Lucien. I recognized a guard who used to alternate with him at the gate. He was usually tough, and abusive but having nothing more to fear, I ventured to ask him casually, "What happened to the young guard they called Booby?"

He looked at me sideways and in a matter-of-fact voice devoid of any emotion he said, "The one at the gate, Booby? Yes, we got word about him last week that he was killed in action on the Russian front. He is better off anyway. We'll probably all be taken prisoners by the Russians. They are not far away." He uttered the words without a sign of regret or pity. Nothing, he was just another casualty of war. Death was accepted as part of life, the price you pay for the Fatherland.

My heart stopped beating for a moment. A great emptiness overcame me, and I felt a terrible sadness. I kept thinking of this decent and sensitive young man. Lucien should have lived, but Hitler's madness had taken its toll on everybody—the good and the bad, the innocent and the guilty. Lucien was dead. He died defending a country he did not belong to. He came to despise the symbolism and fear his uniform evoked in those he guarded. He gave me a glimmer of a beautiful and kind soul. In my heart, I quietly began to mourn my lovely and gentle young friend.

On May 5th 1945, having survived the endless march, I was liberated by the Russian army somewhere deep in the heart of what was left of Germany and Hitler's Third Reich.

Under a large birch tree with tears in my eyes, I opened the envelope again and read, *In memory of a tragic and yet so enchantingly beautiful time, to you my beloved Nelli... Little girl, can you imagine, how in the stillness of the dark night, my heart is so full of longing for you... little girl, can you imagine? Just ask the stars, they will tell you how my heart is calling for you... just ask the stars...* Verses written with poetic wonder and youthful love. The concluding lines said, *Don't ever lose courage and always be full of hope. You who have suffered beyond endurance will be rewarded for your suffering. The good is yet to come. If it is God's will that I should live, I shall search for you and I shall find you. I love you, Lebewohl!"...*

But Lucien would find me no more. I looked at his photograph and the image of his gentle face. As far as his German comrades were concerned, he was also forgotten.

I wish I had known his last name or the town from which he came. I would have tried to locate his family in Luxembourg to

Wo liegt so fern die schöne Zeit
Da wir so glücklich waren zu zweit!

26. II 1945
Retzow

Zum Andenken an eine
traurige, und doch so berauschend
schöne und glückliche Zeit,
Dir meine kleine Nelly!

Frühlingsabend, deine Stille,
Lässt Gedanken blühn und schäumen
Drängt mein Herz zu leisem träumen
Dir ergeben ohne Wille.

Glutrot strahlend über grünen Felder,
Leuchtend wie ein Riesenbrand,
Wo eben noch die Sonne stand,
Sinkt der Himmel hinter schwarzen Wälder.

Abend, in der Dämmerstunde
Der amsel [...] Lied erklingt
Bis ein erstes Sternlein blinkt
Und der Mond beginnt die Runde.

Nächtlicher Himmel, glitzernde Pracht
Du lässt mich all meine Sorgen vergessen,
Mein Herz hat noch nie was schöneres besessen
Als dich du herrliche Frühlingsnacht!

Und doch bin ich traurig, warum nur, warum?

Kleines Mädchen, kannst Du ahnen,
Wie ich heut in dunkler Nacht
Voll Sehnsucht hab an Dich gedacht,
Kleines Mädchen, kannst du's ahnen?

Lass Dir von den Sternen sagen
Wie mein Herz nach Dir verlangt,
Wie mit jedem Schlag es um dich bangt,
Brauchst nur mal die Sternen fragen!

Und wenn alles bricht, bleib tapfer Mädel, verliere nie
den Mut und denk dass auch in weiter Ferne mein Herz
wird immer für dich schlagen. Wer kennt die Launen
des Schicksals, ein Schicksal das heute hart, vielleicht
morgen schon wieder lacht. [...] werde ich mit neuem Mut
um dich kämpfen, ich werde [...] suchen und werd dich auch
finden! Hab Vertrauen [...] Zukunft! Lebewohl!
Ewig dein Lucien

In memory of a tragic, and yet so enchantingly
beautiful and joyful time, to you my little Nelly.

Spring evening, your solitude,
Lets my memories bloom and shimmer
It stirs my heart to quiet dreams
And lets them flow with abandonment

The glowing sunset, over green fields
Illuminates the sky like a burning fire
Where the sun was just shining, darkness
Has emerged from the Black Forest

The robin sings his joyous song
Until the first little star emerges,
And the moon begins its reign.

Oh, you beautiful glittering night sky,
You let me forget all my worries,
My heart has never felt such beauty
As you, you glorious Spring night!

And yet I am sad, why then, why?

Little girl, can you ever know
How, in the still of the night
Full of longing I think of you,
Little girl, can you ever know?

Speak to the stars, and let them tell you
How my heart is full of longing for you
How with every beat it fears for you.
Just ask the stars!

And when all breaks, remain strong girl, and never lose courage. Always
remember that in the far away fields, my heart will always beat for you.
Who knows the fickleness of fate? Fate that is hard today, will shine on
us and laugh with us again. I will then with renewed strength fight for
you, I will search for you, and I will find you! Have faith in the future.

Lebewohl! Ever yours, Lucien

tell them of their beloved Lucien. He will always live in my memory. Even now, so many years later, his gentle soul and words remain with me. He touched me very deeply with his love and caring.

Comfortably resting in my chair in America many worlds later, as I hold his poem and photograph, my memories travel back to those tragic days in Retzow. Could the guard have been mistaken about Lucien's death? Could he have been taken prisoner? Could he still be alive? I will never know. I only know that I will never forget him. He brought a glimmer of hope and tenderness to me at a time when my world was empty and hopeless. He left me with a glimmer of light amidst a world of darkness. He left me with a sense of wonderment that my capacity for love had not vanished, even in the most unlikely place on earth, surrounded by beasts who walked like men. He will continue to live on in my memory. No, Lucien, I have not forgotten you...

It is human nature to forgive and forget. One cannot forgive mass murder, but one can forgive one individual. And I have forgiven Lucien for "the crime he did not commit".

Chapter 4

Prague

In June 1945, I boarded a bus to Prague. The final destination in the long and uncomfortable three-day journey from Prenzlau was just a few kilometers away. Anticipation was high, and everyone on our bus was anxious to disembark. We were approaching the outskirts of the city and finally, the bus came to a full stop. I felt excited and apprehensive. I had no idea what was to come next.

I traveled to Prague with a group consisting of mostly men and a few women who were former prisoners of war, slave laborers, and concentration camp inmates returning home to their families. During our journey when I was looking out of the window, I could hardly believe a picture of a peaceful, rural pastoral scene of Sudetenland, scattered with small houses, acres of fields and trees, and farm animals roaming and grazing on the grass; a scene I had not witnessed for four years. There was another world after all, an outside world I was going to join, somehow. I was totally unaware how and where I would finally wind up. Four days earlier, I had boarded the bus in Prenzlau, a town liberated by the Soviets in what became East Germany after the war.

Retzow-am-Rechlin, where I was interned for the past four months, having been deported there via Auschwitz and then

Ravensbruck, was evacuated in early May 1945. It was a long and arduous march that seemed endless. We had no idea where we were being taken. There were massive air raids, and the guards, having finally come to terms that this was the end of the Third Reich, lost interest and no longer cared what happened to us. During the march, I became friendly with a few other women, and we kept encouraging each other by talking about liberation. The magic words were: "We have come so far. The war was obviously at an end. Keep your strength up.

For the first time in many years, I started to hope that maybe we could survive the harrowing march to nowhere. I did not know it then, of course, but that section of Germany was totally surrounded on all four sides by the Allies. We could hear the roar of the magnificent guns from far away. We could see the sky clearly illuminated by the firearms and marvel at the flaming red sky cutting across the frightening dark while we hid in the ditches. For the first time in four years, I heard the echo of another world, a world where people were given the privilege to fight for their freedom.

During the massive bombardments, the guards did not bother to look for us. They now tried to find cover for themselves and left the camp inmates alone. Finally, during the last onslaught when the guards were out of our sight, we spotted an abandoned farm and found shelter in its barn.

I climbed on a ladder to the second level, a vast area covered with straw and hay, and I spent the night listening to the bombs exploding and noises from the cows on the ground floor beneath us. The sound of the bursting bombs never sounded so good!

On May 5, 1945, after days in what seemed like an endless ordeal, we were finally liberated in an unknown little hamlet in an abandoned farm, somewhere in East Germany.

Dawn was approaching; the bombs stopped falling; and the sun shone through the cracks of the barn. I edged to the wall and looked out through the cracks, and I could hardly believe my eyes. Soviet soldiers were standing in the yard with rifles on their shoulders. I woke up the girls and then ran down the ladder into the yard. I practically embraced one of the soldiers. He looked at me as if I came from another world, which of course I had. I spoke to him in Russian that I had learned in Grodno during its two years of Soviet rule from 1939 to 1941. The rest of the girls followed, and the soldiers didn't quite know what to make of us.

One soldier asked me how we got to be in that village and from where had we come. I briefly told him, and I was really shocked when he said, "You are Jewish? I was sure you Jews were all dead. You mean there are some left?" It was not what he said but how he said it. That was my first encounter with a Soviet anti-Semite. The great experiment of the workers' paradise where equality was supposed to have reigned and religion was of no consequence had not really altered the psyche of the Russian people. I was very pained to listen to his tone and implication after all we had just been through. In my total naiveté, I still believed in the "new man" that was "preached" to me during my school days in Grodno. Yet this one military embodiment of the Soviet system clearly showed how centuries-old hatred and anti-Semitism were still being transferred from one ignorant generation to another.

The war was officially declared over on May 8. Since I spoke fluent Russian and German, the captain in charge asked me to act as his interpreter. I will never forget the feeling when I was hoisted into an enormous Katiusha tank with twenty-four unshaven Soviet soldiers who were playing the accordion and guitar and sang their hearts out. They sang a beautiful song called *Officers' Waltz*. The eerie scene and the melody stuck with me forever. Years later when I was walking with a date in Times Square in New York, *Officers' Waltz* was blasting away over the loudspeaker from a record store. I stopped, transported to another time. I was back riding on a Katiusha tank with twenty-four unshaven singing Soviet soldiers. My date didn't know what had happened to me.

For the next number of weeks, the girls and I stayed together at the farm in an abandoned main house; the owners had

probably fled the approaching Soviets. We "transported" ourselves from the barn to the house, and although it contained a
number of different rooms, we all decided to sleep in one room
for safety. We found food on the farm. Although I could have
eaten all I wanted, in actuality, I could eat only very little; my
stomach had shrunk from all the years of starvation.

We felt isolated in this village since there did not appear to
have been anyone except Russian soldiers and a few local farm-
ers. We tried to find out how to get information to reach a repatriation center, but the only way to get anywhere was to be
transported by a military car. The Captain in charge took a
strong liking to me since I was interpreting for him, and I
thought I would find a good opportunity to ask him for help.

The Captain used to send his orderly to fetch me for dinner
at his quarters, and he gave me all kinds of presents that I was
sure he stole from the villages. One evening in a matter of-fact
manner, he announced that he was going to marry me. First, he
was going to send me to the Ukraine to his mother's house, and
I was to wait for him there! "I know you are only sixteen and I
am forty-two, but I will make you a good husband," he
announced. I was horrified. I told him that I was too young to
marry, that I had an aunt in New York and I wanted to go and
be with her. He became furious. He then asked me to return all
the presents he had given me. That was my first marriage proposal. What an episode! Eventually he did provide us with an
army vehicle and had us driven to a place called Prenzlau.

I spent about four weeks in Prenzlau, a city in the
Neubrandeburg district in East Germany about twenty-eight
miles WSW from Stettin (Szczecin) on the Polish-German border. Prenzlau became a center and hub for all refugees. From
there, prisoners of war, slave laborers, and concentration camp
survivors could be repatriated to their various countries. During
that time, I met a Belgian ex-prisoner of war who was going
home to Brussels. He asked me if I had any relatives, and I told
him that I had an aunt in New York. He asked me if I knew her
address and name. I told him her name is Anna Kleban, and I

gave him her address. My mother made me memorize her address before we were all separated in Grodno. He promised to write to her and let her know that I was alive. He did as he promised, writing that we met by chance in Prenzlau. I was amazed that in our early correspondence when I was in Prague he wrote to my aunt at length of my survival. His letter was the first time she had any knowledge that I was alive. My aunt was pretty fluent in French, and the two corresponded for a number of years. I still have the first letter he wrote to her.

My "angel" Martha and I were separated when Auschwitz was being evacuated to a number of different concentration camps deeper inside Germany to flee from the advancing Soviet army. I was sent to Ravensbruck, a camp built for 3,000 and packed in that January 1945 with 20,000. What an extraordinary confluence and unbelievable coincidence that Martha and I found each other among the thousands of people in that cradle of horror. We embraced and shed tears of joy to see each other again. We talked and somehow hoped that maybe we could survive before the war ended.

Knowing that there was no one left from my family and there was no one to go home to, I had no intention of returning to my hometown. Martha said, "If either of us survives, I want you to come to Zilina and I will look after you."

I stayed in Ravensbruck for three weeks, and once again I was evacuated to yet another camp. Martha and I were separated. I did not know where she was taken and I wound up in Retzow-am-Rechlin. What she told me in Ravensbruck stuck in my mind. After our liberation on May 8, 1945, my only thought was to go to Zilina, the town in Czechoslovakia where she was from. Of course I had no idea where that was but I knew that I first had to go to Prague.

In my "University of Auschwitz," I learned a number of other languages while interacting with so many women from so many different countries. I had a natural knack for languages; they came easily to me. In addition to Polish, Russian and

French, I became quite fluent in German, Slovak, and Hungarian (people in Slovakia spoke Hungarian as well as Slovak, which is different from Czech).

Having acquired a good knowledge of those languages became very useful. When I was finally "processed" at the Prentzlau repatriation center, I lied about my age. I told them that I was a year older and that I was born in Zilina. When they spoke to me in Slovak and Hungarian, I was apparently quite persuasive. And that is how I wound up being placed on a bus leaving Prentzlau in June 1945—destination Prague.

The driver announced that we were approaching the out-skirts of Prague, just a few kilometers away. I felt excited and strange, but I was not afraid. I had no idea what awaited me. Even then, without being aware of it, I naively believed in fate, luck, and hope. These may have been the very qualities that sustained me. I was disembarking from a four-day bus trip in a strange country, not speaking Czech and not knowing if Martha had ever gone to Zilina.

Still, I was hoping for the best when the bus finally arrived at our destination. People embraced and wished each other good luck, and I got off the bus with the others. I stepped on the pavement and found myself surrounded by people who came to greet my fellow travelers. I stood aside watching the emotional reunions, knowing that nobody was waiting for me. For the first time in my life, having found myself in a strange city and with no knowledge of the local language, I was finally faced with the harsh reality of the past four years and the devastating loss of my family. I stood alone and a bit confused as to what to do next. What was so painful was the realization that everyone on that bus was met by a family member or a friend. I stood there by myself, struck with the reality that I was really totally alone in the world.

We were told on the bus that those traveling to other parts of Czechoslovakia (Slovakia was then part of it) could obtain tickets free of charge. I was also advised that I should spend the night at the Jan Masaryk House before taking the train the next morning. I was given directions to the train station and obtained my train ticket to Zilina. After I received my ticket on my way out of the station, I suddenly realized that I could not remember the name of the place where I was supposed to spend the night. I had no idea who Jan Masaryk was. I found out later that he was a politician and the son of the former Prime Minister of Czechoslovakia, a name well known and highly respected by the Czech people.

Well, I thought, *I will just have to find a place and wait somewhere until the next morning.* The afternoon was warm and comfortable. I kept walking and found myself in a park, Vaclavske Namiesto. I decided to wait it out there, sitting on a bench with lovely trees and flowers around. Nobody was standing over me with a gun or a whip, and nobody was yelling in German. I was not frightened. Today I can imagine how I must have looked: a young girl with long blond hair holding on to a little white sweater around her shoulders and clutching a little bag with all her earthly belongings!

Shortly after I made myself comfortable at my bench, a young man approached me and sat down next to me. He looked at me, puzzled, and asked what I was doing there sitting all alone. We spoke in German. I briefly told him my story. Once again, luck and fate intervened. The young man's name was Vaclav Ruziczka, and I will never forget him. He was probably in his mid-20s, and he took an interest in me. The first question he asked me was, "You have traveled all this distance to come here and then you want to travel on to Zilina. Are you sure your friend is waiting for you there?"

"No," I said, "I have no idea if she survived or if she went to Zilina."

We talked for some time and then he asked me if I had any family anywhere. "Yes," I said, "I have an aunt, my mother's sister, who lives in New York City."

"Do you know her address?" he continued. I told him that my mother made me memorize it. "You know," he said, "if you

Vaclav Ruziczka

remain in Prague you could try to write to her and let her know that you are alive. Would you like me to help you?" At that time, the only way to send mail to America was through American soldiers. "I am sure if you give your letter to one, he will probably send it for you. I can take you to a Catholic Charity House where you could stay until you can find out what to do next."

Once again, life and death decisions were made without hesitation. "Alright, I will go with you, and I will also see if at some point I can find out about Martha." I was so hopelessly naïve. Of course he could have taken me astray, but I trusted him. Vaclav turned out to be a real friend, and we corresponded for many years after I had left Prague. I spent three months living at the charity house, looked after by the nuns who were compassionate and kind.

I wrote five identical letters in Russian to my aunt. At the bottom of each I added, "Please don't think I have lost my mind writing the exact letters, but I am giving each to an American soldier and I am not sure if any or all will reach you." Vaclav helped me with this project. A month or so later, I received a telegram from my aunt. She had received all five letters and was thrilled to hear from me and to know where I was. Since the time when the Belgian gentleman wrote to her about me, she had tried to get information on the whereabouts of me and any member of our family. She was advised that they could find no one from our family in Grodno. She accepted the reality that none of her relatives had survived. And the authorities could not find me since I was "processed" as having been born in Zilina, Czechoslovakia.

During my stay at the Catholic Charity House, I learned enough Czech and was given a job at a large typewriter firm where Vaclav's father held an important position. A few months later, Vaclav also found another lodging for me at a special residence for young ladies who came to work or study in Prague and whose families made sure they had a safe and pleasant place to live. At the time I was earning a salary and was even able to make a monetary contribution toward my upkeep.

My aunt and I corresponded as best we could because mail was still very sketchy. She assured me that as soon as it was possible, she would send a visa. In the meantime, she and her friends sent me wonderful packages of goodies that I always shared with the people in the office. I could not figure out why a little bag filled with tea had a string attached to it. What a waste to tear it open and put the tea in a brewing pot. Finally, someone at the office who spoke a little English said that one simply had to submerge the bag directly into the cup, and the tea would brew itself! *How strange America is*, I thought.

I had been staying in Prague for eight months when I was approached by the American Joint Distribution Committee. (I am not sure how they found me. It was probably through my aunt.) They suggested that I should go to London and wait for my visa there. I went for an interview with the American military representative; I told him that I really didn't want to go to London but to New York instead. He replied, "You will eventually go to New York but it may take some time since you are on the Polish visa quota. There is a long waiting list. In the meantime you can go to London and start learning English."

"Alright," I said. Once again, major life decisions were made at the drop of a hat.

Amazingly during my stay in Prague, Martha somehow found me. She had never gone to Zilina, but she wound up with members of her family in Stettin (Szczecin), the city on the Polish-German border near the Prenzlau repatriation center from which I had traveled to Prague. So once again, it was a lucky confluence that I never went to Zilina. Martha arranged for me to visit her in Stettin, and she sent her nephew who was in the Czech army to take me there. Martha apparently had an extensive family who had immigrated to Brazil shortly before the war broke out, and she was soon planning to join them in São Paulo. She wanted to adopt me and was hoping that she could eventually send for me. I did not want to go anywhere except to New York to be with the only remaining member of my family, and she understood that.

I visited Martha in São Paolo in 1967. She had married soon after she arrived, probably in 1947. I met her lovely family who were well situated and lived in lovely homes. Unfortunately, her husband died before I had a chance to meet him. There is no question that I owe a great part of my survival to this kind and remarkable lady. She nurtured me when I was deathly sick; she gave me encouragement and hope during intense suffering when it was very difficult to give strength to anyone; and she looked after me as though she were my mother.

There are incidents in one's life that are deeply embedded and stand out so clearly in one's mind. One such incident was of course Vaclav, having quite by chance found me one late afternoon sitting on a bench in Prague's Vaclavske Namiesto during the middle of June 1945. It must have a special meaning. Was it providence? Who knows? I wonder sometimes what would have happened had I continued on my journey to Zilina the next morning. I am glad I never knew. I have no idea where I would have gone next since I would have been even more isolated in a smaller town without knowing a soul.

Vaclav gave me a personal memento, a medallion of the Madonna with the infant Jesus, for good luck before I left for London. I still have it and cherish the part he played in my life. We corresponded for a number of years, and he sent me a lovely photograph of his marriage. It depicted Vaclav and his beautiful bride wearing a traditional Czech headdress, holding a lovely bouquet of flowers. Next to Vaclav stood his dignified father and seated was the bride's youthful mother. The photo has been hanging on my wall for all these years.

We corresponded in Czech, and I wrote to him from London. He gave me the news about Prague and the people with whom I became friendly in his father's office. It was nice to hear about the life I had left behind, if it had only been for nine months. Unfortunately, in 1948, Czechoslovakia fell under the domination of the Soviet Union. Had I remained in Prague after 1948, I would have been stuck there, and I would not have been able to leave either for London or New York. The borders were sealed. Somebody up there was looking after me.

Vaclav and I eventually lost touch with each other but he meant so much to me. I will be eternally grateful that fate intervened once again, and I was so fortunate that Vaclav touched my life at such a crucial time. Like Martha, he was one of my special angels.

Chapter 5

London

The send-off from the friends I had made during my nine months in Prague was very touching. The typewriter-factory office staff, with whom I had worked for six of those months, presented me with a lovely gift. A *bon voyage* party at a friend's house was held in my honor with genuine expressions of "good luck" and "don't forget us." Vaclav was encouraging and continued to give me moral support; he promised to write. His special gift of the little medallion of the Madonna holding the infant Jesus was tucked away in my purse.

The following morning on March 1, 1946 I boarded a British Army plane (with bucket seats) on the flight to London, along with a transport of children from Czechoslovakia. We were actually supposed to have left the day before, but the fog over the English Channel was so heavy that nothing was flying.

This was my first time on a airplane. It took four hours before we finally touched ground, and the flight proved to be a real challenge for me. The weather was bad, and the flight was bumpy. I was very airsick. At that time, the thought of ever flying again made me cringe with fear.

Ever since I first landed in London a month before my seventeenth birthday, I have felt a very strong bond with England. As is often typical of English weather, the day was rainy, foggy, and dreary, but none of that mattered. I felt wonderfully excited and glad to be off the plane! The feeling of euphoria kept creeping in, and I knew that my life was taking on a new and meaningful course. Prague was the beginning and England was the continuation on the journey to self-awakening and to new challenges.

I have often wondered how a surge of hope and joy could spring up within me when a situation looked so uncertain and, realistically, I had little reason to feel particularly euphoric. I was not sure where I was going; I did not know anyone in this new land; and I knew exactly three English words: "Thank You" and "Please." In fact, I didn't know anything except that I was alive and in a civilized country! I knew I had to adjust to life outside the camps, to learn a new language again, and eventually to get a job and become a productive member of society. I was cognizant that I would have to readjust to a new environment and learn to cope with freedom in a foreign land, all alone. But then, everything was foreign to me.

Years later, in retrospect, when I started to come to terms with my survival, to understand and analyze my weaknesses and strengths, I realized that in moments of stress I tended to become calm, as if my body was telling me to conserve my emotional energy. I lived with optimism and hope, in total defiance of reality. But that defiance was an important defense mechanism. To understand one's survival and move on with life was a way to set aside the memories of devastating experiences and look toward the future, uncertain as that future might have been at that time. I was blessed with unfailing optimism.

Of course, there was no logic in trying to find a reason for the terrible suffering. During my years in Auschwitz and the camps afterward, I used to revert into my inner self and enter my private world of fantasy to find the strength to go on. That feeling afforded me an escape from the harsh reality and an entry into my own private little world of dreams for a few brief moments. I would try to push aside the negative thoughts that fell into definable patterns and try to change the negativism into a positive energy. I kept thinking of my sister's encouraging words. All that helped to keep me sane.

Lifetimes later during my psychology courses at the University of Pennsylvania, I studied Freud's defense mechanisms: sublimation resembled my mental state. Of course, I was completely unaware of all that back then. I was always amazed that this positive energy served me well during my adult years when, on a day I was to perform in an opera or concert, I would feel lethargic, tired, and wondering how I could possibly face the audience feeling so listless and "blah." Then remarkably, just before I came on stage, my adrenaline started flowing and released my stored up energy. I felt completely energized and ready to face the audience.

On the way to the London hostel where we were to stay for a while until other accommodations were found, I kept looking out the window of the car. I was in awe of the shops displaying lovely ware; the symmetry of the row homes with their manicured lawns and shrubbery; and the tall buildings. I observed with interest how people dressed, the bustle of the city, the funny looking double-decker buses full of advertisements that I could not yet understand, and the odd-looking taxicabs! Everything seemed magical, and I felt like a true country bumpkin full of wonderment.

We arrived at an undistinguished brick building, and we were greeted by friendly representatives who made us feel welcome. I stayed in the hostel for a few weeks, and then I was taken to my "temporary permanent home," as it was explained to me, the lovely estate of Whitlars in Hartfordshire, about an hour's drive from London. The estate once belonged to a lady who had donated it to a Jewish agency for housing young refugees just arriving from abroad.

The house itself was quite spacious, surrounded with stately trees. The grounds were full of lush shrubbery and manicured flowerbeds so typical of stately English homes. I shared a bedroom with two other girls with whom I had become quite friendly.

Dolly spoke German, and Silvia spoke Hungarian. To my recollection, the estate housed about sixteen young people from a number of different countries, all speaking their native tongues. Fate was taking care of me again, and I went with the flow. My exhaustive English vocabulary, that had consisted of three words upon my arrival soon grew to at least twenty words.

One incident stands out during my residence at Whitlars because it brought me my first encounter with live orchestral music on a grand scale. Music was in my blood and had always been a part of me. I came from a musical family, and as a child, my musical ability, particularly in singing, manifested itself quite early.

From Whitlars, we were taken one evening by bus to the Royal Albert Hall to hear the London Symphony Orchestra, featuring Arthur Rubinstein, perform Rachmaninoff's Second Piano Concerto. The evening turned out to be an exciting and totally new experience. First I was in awe of the grandeur of the hall itself. Then the majestic opening bars sent an absolute shiver through me and left an indelible impression up to this day. Even now whenever I hear the opening bars of the concerto, I become emotionally charged. I had never heard that music before, and piano was always an instrument I was strongly drawn to.

My eldest cousin, Sara, had studied piano at the Warsaw Conservatory, and she was just beginning her concert career when the war broke out. (She alone among my extended family managed to survive the war in Almaty, playing piano for the Kazakhstan Ballet. She now lives in retirement in Tel Aviv. As a child, I would look eagerly forward to visiting Sara's house whenever she came home from Warsaw. Then I would hide under their grand piano and listen to the wonderful sounds emanating from Chopin's glorious music.

The drive back on the bus from the concert was delayed because the driver was waiting for "the pea soup fog" to lift before we could proceed. I could not have cared less. I settled comfortably in my seat, closed my eyes, and savored the glorious sounds of Rachmaninoff's Second Piano Concerto and

Rubinstein's performance. I was apparently oblivious to everything around me; my friends kept asking me if I was alright, and all I could say was that I was still listening to the music.

While I lived in protected surroundings and was well taken care of, I also recognized, even at that early stage, that I had to get hold of my life and find my own way. Living comfortably at Whitlars was not going to advance my life. I was concentrating on learning and absorbing English as fast as I could because I recognized that without knowing the language, I could not make headway. I even started to write in English. In one of my letters to my aunt in New York, I tried to write, "I cannot yet write English, but in the future I hope I shall can." "I cannot yet but in the future I will be able to," somehow made no sense to me.

Without analyzing or understanding as the expression often used today "to find out who I am," I felt that only I could make things happen. If I were going to master English and start life on my own, London would be the place. I recognized that without solid knowledge of the language (something I was determined to achieve as soon as possible), I would never get anywhere. I needed to be around people who spoke only English, and at Whitlars we continued to speak our native languages. I took matters into my own hands and managed to get information about relocating to London and getting a job. I was the first at Whitlars to leave after six months and move to London. With the help of a Board member, I obtained a small room with a family in the Kensington section of London.

During my stay at Whitlars, we were given psychological and physical tests to determine if special help might be appropriate after our ordeal. I had a session with a lovely lady psychologist. While I enjoyed talking with her, I was surprised how neatly she tried to put everything into a certain perspective. Every question and my expected answers were categorized as though they were going to be put in little boxes, as though life could be arranged that simply.

Years later, in my studies at Penn and then in my studies for my Master's degree, we explored different approaches and disciplines within the field of psychology dealing with human communication. I was amazed how many different schools of psychology there were and I wondered how someone chose one approach over another.

Honesty and inner pain are essential emotions that are needed to overcome psychological discomforts, and analysis starts within oneself. I believe that psychiatrists often use a guessing game. They latch on to an event in a person's life and elaborate on that aspect. When you deal with painful memories, especially recent memories, there is no set pattern of determination. I actually enjoyed talking to the Whitlars psychologist, and she obviously enjoyed my visit too. She commented as we parted that I was brave, alert, and had a realistic view of life. No, she did not think I needed subsequent visits, thank you.

Soon after I moved into my comfortable little room in Kensington, I obtained a job working for *The Jewish Monthly*, a prestigious and intellectually oriented magazine. The publication was concerned with promoting mutual understanding and goodwill between Christians and Jews in all sectors of the community and with fostering greater co-operation between Christians and Jews to combat religious and racial intolerance. (In the years to come, I became actively involved in the cause of promoting greater understanding between Christians and Jews. I spoke to many churches, civic groups, colleges, and universities on the subject.)

My job at *The Jewish Monthly* consisted of relatively insignificant office duties and also of answering the phone. I found my duties a bit problematic because, having been in London only seven months and obviously not born speaking perfect English, it was an absolutely scary task. Although my English was getting pretty fluent, attempting to understand men who spoke while smoking a cigar and often mumbling into the phone was really quite frightening.

In Auschwitz, I tried to keep a diary in my head. When I came to Prague, I started to write my recollections in Polish. While working for *The Jewish Monthly*, with the help of a friend, I started to translate some of my writings into English. I showed it to the editor, and he felt that what I had written was an important and significant historical human document worthy of publication. *A Day in Auschwitz* was published in the August 1947 edition of *The Jewish Monthly*. It was very well received.

During the ensuing months, my life took on a sense of normalcy. My social circle was expanding; I was meeting new people; and I was also dating. Cyril, a charming man whose family lived in Cardiff, invited me to spend a weekend with his family. Cyril proudly escorted me around Cardiff and showed off the beautiful Welsh countryside.

When I arrived in England, I was called by my given name which was Nelli (pronounced with a soft "L"). Cyril is responsible for re-naming me. He said, "You know, the way people pronounce Nelli in England is harsh and not the soft way you say it; Nelly for some reason is often a name given to a cow. You certainly don't show the slightest resemblance to that! You look like a Ninochka, and I will call you Nina from now on." Well, it did stick, and everyone started calling me Nina. I made the name official when I arrived in America.

I kept reading a lot and tried to devour books on as many subjects as I could understand. I loved going to the theatre and to the cinema, and I went as often as possible. Each time I went, I learned a new sentence, and my vocabulary kept improving. I was beginning to speak with a real British intonation, so I was told.

Things were looking up. Eventually, I got a bigger room with another family in the Hampstead section of London. I also changed jobs and was now working for a German dentist, who was a refugee from Berlin. Dr. Kuttner and his family were kind and lovely people, and we became good friends. We all had a good laugh when he read one of my messages. "Mrs. Brown called for an early appointment because she lost her feelings."

Well, I soon learned to differentiate "feelings" from "fillings," especially in a dental office!

Whenever I would wear a short-sleeved dress, the grotesque tattooed number on my left forearm stood out rather prominently. One day a young girl on a bus turned to me and inquired, "What kind of a prison were you in? I never saw that before!"

When I was tattooed in January 1943, the numbers were large and covered a large portion of the left forearm. I very rarely talked about my recent past, and I was not comfortable talking about it. I didn't want to feel like a marked woman. I felt very strongly that if possible, I wanted to have the number permanently removed.

The opportunity presented itself when a friend of Dr. Kuttner mentioned a plastic surgery center in Greenwich. An appointment was made for me, and I was very fortunate to be referred to Dr. McIndoe, who was a pioneer in the field of early British reconstructive plastic surgery. The hospital was essentially built to treat members of the British armed forces, especially the RAF pilots who were severely burned and injured. Many men spent a number of years in the hospital undergoing massive grafting. It was in this hospital that Dr. McIndoe removed my tattoo under local anesthesia. When he looked at my forearm, he told me that he had never removed a tattoo before, and he was concerned that the scar would most likely be quite deep and prominent. He asked me to come back in six months to correct the surgery and make the scar much smaller. I told him that it did not matter how big the scar was, as long as the tattoo was gone.

While I worked as a dental assistant for Dr. Kuttner, I met Herman Simberg, one of the doctor's patients, a flamboyant and charming man, who was a former opera and concert singer and a well-known voice teacher in London. He would often engage me in conversation and wanted to know more about me. He had an active voice studio, and among his students were many stage and film actors. On one occasion, he said something that struck me as

Nina and Aunt Anita
London – 1948

funny, and I laughed out loud. He looked at me seriously and asked, "You have such a beautiful melodic laugh! Do you sing?"

I told him that I have always been singing, and I was also studying the piano. He asked me to come to his studio and said that he wanted to hear me sing. I sang for him, accompanying myself on the piano. He immediately offered to teach me on a full scholarship. I studied with Simberg about six months before I left London for New York. It was the beginning of my serious vocal studies.

As our lessons progressed, he had great hopes for me and was very encouraging. He also suggested that I think about a movie career; he actually arranged an audition with a scout from one of the big film studios. Apparently the scout was impressed because he wanted to introduce me to the studio heads. But that happened a few weeks before I was to leave for New York. I had waited four years for a US visa and now I had one! Nothing could have dissuaded me from my dream of going to America. Possibly, had I stayed in London, I might have actually had a chance of becoming an actress.

My time to leave for New York was approaching, and Simberg decided to give me a special send-off before I left London. Without saying a word to me, he secretly called one of my "beaus" and the two of them "plotted" and arranged to hold a party in his spacious studio. It was to be a combination birthday and farewell affair. He invited many of his well-known actor and musician friends as well as my own circle of friends. It was carefully planned and elegantly catered. I wrote to my aunt to tell her that I was actually invited to my own farewell/birthday party!

During the evening, everyone was asked to participate and perform. I too was asked to sing. The party was a great success, and it was written up in a few London papers and in *Sound*, a widely read theatrical magazine for which Russell Palmer was the highly respected music critic. The May 1950 issue featured Danny Kaye on the cover and also Palmer's review:

"I have often thought it a pity that the Victorian custom which insisted that everyone play or sing something at a party should have

"gone out" of fashion. When artists get together, they revive the true party spirit. They each perform to entertain the others—not always in the sphere of entertainment for which they are known to the public.

Many well known celebrities were among those present at a all-night party in Hampstead, presided over by that genial and combustible host, the tenor, Herman Simberg, to celebrate a charming pupil's 21st birthday.

The young lady whose birthday we celebrated, Nina Kaleska from Poland, had a terrible ordeal in German hands during the war. She is training her voice under Simberg, and she is leaving for America soon. She sings a great variety of material, accompanying herself at the piano. It is an extremely sweet voice, soft, persuasive, expressive. I think she has a big future…a successful party indeed!"

On another occasion, a well-known portrait artist, Mabel Messer, who was also a patient of Dr. Kuttner, took great interest in me. Every time she would come for treatment, she kept looking at me and smiling. Finally she said, "You have such an interesting face. Would you allow me to paint you?" Dr. Kuttner encouraged me to accept her invitation. I posed for her for a few months. When the painting was finished she said, "I have used the same background for you as I have for Winston Churchill." The painting turned out lovely and was quite large and impressively framed. A number of people offered to buy it but she said she would hold it for me for a while until I could buy it from her. In the event of her death, she promised to leave it to me in her will. Unfortunately and unexpectedly, she died shortly thereafter, and I did not have enough money to purchase it from her brother.

A few months before I left for New York, I was introduced to a remarkable man. It was a blind date arranged by a mutual friend; I had a serious crush on our mutual friend. Since he was involved with a well-known actress, he arranged for his friend Bob to meet me. Bob was a successful lawyer, writer, and intellect. The first time we met he picked me up in a gray Bentley convertible, and he was dressed in a casual English suit. He was tall and thin with an interesting face, but I did not think him particularly handsome. He was always attentive, polite, and a perfect gentleman. "England is a beautiful country," he said. "Let me show you some of it before you leave for the 'jungle of New York'."

He took me to the Tower of London and recounted the fascinating but gory history that went with it. It was strange that in the four years I had been living in London, I had never been there. Now with Bob as my escort extraordinaire, I became a tourist, going to places and doing things tourists did, and I loved it. We would drive two hours out of London to the countryside and eat lunch in a pub built in the twelfth century. I was totally fascinated by his exquisite use of the English language and his extensive knowledge of history, architecture, and literature. He knew a lot about music and particularly liked Mozart.

I had also by that time acquired considerable knowledge about music, and I fell in love with Beethoven. We had heated discussions about the two musical giants. Bob was also passionate about the ballet, and we had two, long-standing front-row seats at Saddler's Wells at Covent Garden. He took me to the ballet every week, and I was fortunate to see the great ballet dancers of the time, including the legendary Margot Fonteyn. I was getting a full dose of ballet history. It was fascinating.

Bob was twelve years older than I. He realized, of course, that I was greatly lacking in knowledge on many levels, and he took great pain in sharing his extensive knowledge about many subjects with me. We saw each other very often. I became an eager pupil, and he enjoyed the part of the teacher. It also became quite obvious that he was quite enamored with me, and one evening over dinner, he proposed marriage. I respected him highly, but I was not in love with him. "Why are you going to the jungle?" he would often ask. "You ought seriously to consider staying here. You know how I feel about you. We could be very happy; you could have a beautiful life. I know you are not in love with me yet, but I am sure in time you will realize how right we are for each other."

Strange, that in all these years and out of the many proposals I have since received, I still think of Bob often with great affection and nostalgia. I simply did not understand the depth and beauty of the man. I was just learning how to face life, and I was really quite naïve and unworldly. Bob spoke to me on a different emotional level of our future together, a future for which I was not quite ready. He overwhelmed me too soon. I was twenty-one and not ready for that kind of a life-long commitment. I somehow think that had I not left for New York and instead stayed in London, our future together would have materialized.

We corresponded for a few months after my departure. His letters were extraordinary, full of poetic phrases, wisdom, and longing...

He stated quite plainly in one letter, "You asked me whether, if you had stayed here, we would have got along. The answer to that isn't very difficult... If you had wanted to stay here, we would have more than got along. You know I want you still, and here comes the tricky part of this letter. I could say to you, 'Chuck America and come back here,' and possibly you might be prepared to do something about it, I would be overjoyed. But then I feel that this might not be fair to you.... Do you wish to come back here? I ask you this once to be utterly frank with me, please. If you do want to return, I will try and do something about it without any strings attached, so that you may be free to make up your mind about me without any question of gratitude or other such feeling to influence your decision. Try to appreciate that all I want is your best happiness. I am most anxious about you..."

Before I left, Bob offered to buy my portrait painted by Mabel Messer, and he promised to send it to me. He did buy it, but apparently he decided to keep it for himself. I know he was still hoping that my stay in New York would not last and that I would change my mind and return to England... Such a future was obviously not to be. To his last letter, perhaps regretfully, I responded by saying that I had decided to remain in America, in terms that must have left no doubt. With that, our correspondence abruptly ceased; Bob never wrote me again.

Chapter 6

The Atlantic

On June 24, 1950, I was standing on the platform of Victoria Station in London waiting for the train to take me to Dover where I was to board the majestic Queen Elizabeth on my voyage to the "Promised Land". I was surrounded by many friends who had come to see me off and wish me well. Once again, my friend Bob, whom I dated for the last four months, tried very hard to dissuade me from leaving civilized England for the "jungle" of New York. Bob was a very private man and he held back his emotions, but his eyes revealed his feelings.

Everyone made a prediction for my "exciting" future, and they gave advice on how to avoid being mugged and survive in New York. My voice teacher Simberg predicted a great career. I was teary-eyed and filled with feelings of nostalgia and strong emotions when I saw the train approaching the platform. The time had come to say goodbye. It was a time to be hugged, kissed, and embraced again. Bob held me closely and quietly whispered "I love you." As nostalgic as I felt, this was the moment I was waiting for since I arrived in England four years ago. I did not realize how deeply attached I became to London emotionally, and secretly, in spite of looking eagerly forward to the journey, I felt very sad to say goodbye.

A few more embraces, a few more hugs and kisses with tears in my eyes, it was really an extraordinary moment. I finally boarded the train and waived my good-byes from the window as the train slowly pulled out of the station on the way to Dover, leaving behind a group of friends who became very special to me... A few hours later, I embarked on the majestic Queen Elizabeth, and I was absolutely in awe of the splendor and classic opulence of the liner. A few hours later we sailed to Cherbourg, France, and we were on the way to the Promised Land.

Sailing from Dover to Cherbourg was exciting. I was meeting my fellow passengers and looking forward to reaching New York five days later. All was wonderful when we left Cherbourg and sailed into the full Atlantic Ocean. On the second day, suddenly, I began to feel the full force of *mal de mer.* For almost three days, I was confined to my bunk and fed ginger ale, which I was told was good for me. I could not eat, and that drink was all I could swallow. Concerned staff assured me that the ginger ale would "cure" me. Well, of course it did not, but I drank the stuff anyway. I could not lift my head, and the room was swirling around me. I felt as though I was going to die. All I wanted to do was to get off the boat! Many years come to pass before I could drink ginger ale again.

At 3:00 AM on June 29, the final day of our voyage, there was a slight knock on my cabin door, and the steward whispered, "We will be shortly approaching New York harbor. You wanted to see the Statue of Liberty." Yes! I jumped out of my lower berth, and I was suddenly filled with a sense of tremendous excitement. I ran to join the other passengers and found my way to the bridge of this great ship.

Standing at the railing, I waited in semi-darkness for the sight of that beautiful French lady holding the eternal torch to welcome me, the Statue of Liberty. It was such a glorious symbol of hope and freedom, and it held such comfort for new arrivals, particularly for those who have experienced oppression. I felt euphoric, apprehensive, and full of joy all mingled together. I was finally reaching the shores of America, the land of the thousands of glimmering fighter planes that flew so high

Hello America
Nina – Queen Elizabeth – June 29, 1950

in the clear blue skies in April 1945 over the remains of Hitler's Third Reich.

Ever since I was abruptly separated from my family and my childhood in Grodno, I had no home and lived where I did not establish permanent roots. Everything seemed temporary. I made an effort to adapt to different environments and situations. I learned new languages and adapted to new cultures. I tried to fit into any group, and I was surprised how easily I managed to adapt. I had made many friends and had serious marriage proposals, but I never really felt at home.

I felt rootless, belonging to everyone and to no one. I was home everywhere and nowhere. Ever since I was separated from my family, I felt that my new home would be in America with my aunt. That dream was about to happen.

Later that day as we were docking and as I was walking toward the exit, I felt a touch on my shoulder, and a man asked me if I was Nina Kaleska. For a moment my heart stopped beating. Perhaps my visa was not in order or something else went wrong.

The young steward recognizing my fear put my mind at ease by telling me that the press was waiting for me with the other celebrities on the first class deck. I had no idea what he was talking about. Why would anyone from the press be interested in talking to me? I followed him, wondering what it was all about. As we approached the deck, a number of photographers and reporters surrounded me. I was treated with deference, and suddenly, here I was amid many celebrities; I still could not understand why I was singled out and what was happening.

Apparently, reporters from the United Press International Syndicate had read the articles about me in the London papers, particularly the review by Russell Palmer, and they thought I would make good copy. What with my unlikely survival and promising talent according to that London critic, I was probably on my way to the Metropolitan Opera!

The following day, most newspapers in New York and the international editions of *The New York Times* and *The Herald*

Tribune featured photographs of Major General William Donovan; a distinguished war hero; the wartime Director of the Office of Strategic Services—the precursor to the CIA—and me. The large photograph and caption read: "Arrivals on the Queen Elizabeth". *The New York Post* headlined: "High Notes at Home and Abroad", and printed photos of another distinguished passenger, the actress Dorothy Lamour—and me.

"The Queen Elizabeth brought a couple of comely and shapely singers here today when it arrived from London," wrote *The Post*. "One is Polish-born Nina Kaleska, 21, who got her first break when a voice teacher heard her laugh while working as a receptionist in a London dentist's office. The other [in parentheses] on the right is Dorothy Lamour who entertained troops in Germany after a two-month personal appearance tour of London and Glasgow."

Miss Lamour was a beautiful and charming lady, but I am not sure she appreciated second billing. She was, after all, a world famous personality—and nobody had ever heard of me!

While the photographers were snapping hundreds of pictures, the reporters kept throwing questions at me such as, "Miss Kaleska, what do you think about the Korean War?" Korean War? What Korean War? I had no idea where Korea was! During our voyage between June 24 and 29, the Korean War had broken out, and of course, I was totally clueless. Nevertheless I responded, "I don't know too much about it yet, but if you would like to ask me again in a week or so, I would be happy to give you my opinion!" The word *chutzpah* comes to mind.

In retrospect, had I been "ready" for an operatic career, the opportunities would have been enormous. I had a million dollars worth of free publicity. And so began the rather auspicious and intriguing interlude of my arrival in New York.

My excitement was mounting, and I couldn't wait to throw my arms around my Aunt Anita. I had met her just once before in 1948 when she came to visit me in London.

Since I was among the last passengers to come ashore, my aunt was beginning to think that perhaps I missed the boat! She was anxiously looking for me while watching the other passengers disembark into the harbor platform on Pier 54, but there was no Nina! Her friends who accompanied her told me later that she was beginning to feel very concerned. They too were eagerly waiting to meet me and welcome me to America.

I finally appeared. We embraced, cried, and laughed; and it was all so wonderful! My aunt was a remarkable lady, and she was also known for her great sense of humor. When I explained the reason why I was late coming off the boat and why other passengers waved to me after leaving the boat, she remarked, "I wouldn't expect anything less of my niece than to rub shoulders with General Donovan and Dorothy Lamour. May I still touch you?"

Chapter 7

New York

After the emotional and touching reunion with my aunt, I settled into her apartment. A steady string of her devoted friends came to see "the miracle girl" they had been hearing about for five years. Sharing the apartment with my aunt was only temporary because it was small. We found a room for me with a sweet elderly lady just two blocks from my aunt's apartment on Central Park West and 105th Street. I paid nine dollars a week for rent.

The publicity about me in the newspapers also generated a response from a number of opera conductors. A few asked to meet me and wondered, when my aunt answered the phone, if Miss Kaleska spoke English. "Yes, Miss Kaleska speaks English very well indeed," was the answer. I was invited to audition for a few; I tried to explain that I was eager to resume studying voice in New York but was not ready for a professional career, at least not yet. At that point I actually had less than six months of formal lessons.

A few months after my arrival in New York, I met Helen Miller Davis. Helen came from a prominent and wealthy New York family. She was shy and soft spoken; she said to me, "I understand that you are interested in studying voice. I know your background and am aware that financially it would be difficult for you at this time to pay for your lessons. I would be happy if you would allow me to help you with your studies." It was the way she said it that made me feel as though I would be giving *her* the privilege in helping *me*. The relationship of Helen's family to mine had begun many years before…

In 1946 while in London, I received a book from Carrie Davidson, the widow of my great uncle, Professor Israel Davidson. I was introduced to Helen in the New York home of Carrie Davidson. The title of the book Carrie Davidson had sent me was *Out of Endless Yearning*, the biography of my great uncle written by her, his devoted wife. Dr. Israel Davidson was a distinguished Professor of Medieval Jewish literature and poetry at The Jewish Theological Seminary of America. The inscription read, "To my grand niece, an introduction to her family". It really *was* an introduction to my family since I never knew any of my grandparents, great aunts, or great uncles, who had all died long before I was born. The biography depicted the odyssey of a man from humble beginnings to recognition as a world-renowned Jewish scholar.

Professor Israel Davidson's compilation of four volumes of the *Thesaurus of Medieval Hebrew Poetry and Literature* became a fundamental work of reference for all future scholarship in the field. He surveyed the creations of more than 2,800 poets, compiling an inventory of 35,000 sacred and secular compositions from the close of the Biblical canon to the beginnings of the Era of Enlightenment. Professor Davidson died in 1939, and sadly, I never met him. His literary works are still studied extensively by scholars of all faiths.

Israel Davidson's parents died before his fifth birthday; he and a younger sister were sent to live in Grodno with an uncle and his wife. The uncle was Rabbi and Cantor Isaac Klebansky, my maternal grandfather. In the late nineteenth century, Grodno and its neighboring communities was a town of about 55,000 with a large Jewish population. It was famous for its Jewish academies and libraries.

Many years later, when my grandfather became widowed, my grandfather married his niece, Davidson's younger sister, who became my grandmother. There was a substantial difference in their ages, but the marriage was happy and produced three daughters: Rebecca, the oldest, my mother; Rachil; and Anna, the youngest. In 1921, Israel Davidson brought his widowed sister, my grandmother, and her unmarried daughter Anna to New York. In America, Anna Klebanska became known as Anita or Anna Kleban, my aunt.

Dr. Louis Finkelstein, then Provost of The Jewish Theological Seminary of America and later as Chancellor, wrote a touching tribute to Israel Davidson. "To those of us who had the privilege of knowing him well, Doctor Davidson often described how he spent his days at college, and at night he earned the pittance necessary to keep body and soul together. When he finally completed his courses at City College with high distinction, he turned for further studies to Columbia University. In spite of countless hardships, Davidson obtained the degree of Doctor of Philosophy in 1902...." When Professor Davidson died, he left among his literary effects a few parting words to be read at his funeral, for he always deplored the ordinary eulogy that made of a man a "white-washed angel" rather than a human being to whom perfection was unattainable.

Perhaps no writing of Doctor Davidson reflected so completely his personality as that read at his funeral in place of a eulogy:

You who have gathered here to take leave of my earthly remains, do not mourn. Death only robs life of its sting. To live and witness our own follies and those of others is the bitterest cup which fate holds to the lip of man. What a relief it is to shake the mortal coil, to be rid of envy, jealousy, hatred, greed, vanity, lust—all the plagues that mortify the flesh. Here I am with you, but no desires gnaw at my heart, and nothing you may have against me affects me. To those who will study my books a hundred years hence I will be as much alive then as I was to those who studied them yesterday. So please do not mourn.

Also, do not waste any of your eloquence on my accomplishments. I would rather tell you some of the weak points in my armor—a sort of Vidui [confessions]—with the object of showing that I too was made of a dual personality, or perhaps a treble personality, i.e., good, bad and indifferent. But I fear such a Vidui would turn out rather a long recital, and if I made you listen to it, I would be committing a greater sin now than I ever committed in my lifetime. So let us pass both praise and blame, let the dust return to dust and let the spirit go on living, free of all mortal entanglements which we erroneously call life.

An interesting confluence and chain of events united me with the remarkable lady who offered to pay for my voice lessons, Helen Miller Davis. It started when Helen's parents, Nathan and Linda Davis, met and became great admirers of Israel Davidson, already a distinguished professor at the Jewish Theological Seminary. Deeply impressed by his scholarship, they offered to sponsor his publication of the *Thesaurus*. Nathan Miller, Helen's father, remarked when asked about his participation in making an important financial contribution, "I do this gladly, for if my name will ever be known to posterity, I believe it will only be through my slight contribution toward this great work." Thus, the publication of *Thesaurus* was launched and, with it, so was a lasting friendship between the Davidsons and the Millers.

Helen Davis became a devoted friend. She sponsored my voice lessons in a way that was so commendable. In order not to involve me, she arranged with my teacher that the bill be sent directly to her, thereby making me feel more comfortable about accepting help. When I tried to express my thanks and appreciation, her answer was, "I am fortunate that through my parents' endowments I am able to help others. It would be my great pleasure to be able to help you. My parents were great admirers of your great uncle and it seems that it is now my turn and privilege to help you." What a unique lady!

In addition to sponsoring my voice lessons for many years, Helen made me feel as though I was part of her family. She was divorced when I met her, and she was the mother of four children. They did not extend to me Helen's friendship. Perhaps they may have felt some resentment because their mother was openly very fond of me.

Helen became very important in my life. She seemed to sense when I needed encouragement. She would telephone and invite me to visit her or take me to the Metropolitan Opera. When I married, Helen insisted on buying me my wedding dress and part of my trousseau. When my older son Ronald was born, she became his godmother. She seemed to need me as much as I needed her. I know it gave her pleasure to care about me. I was very fortunate to know her, and indirectly, I thanked my great uncle and Carrie Davidson for introducing me to her.

In 1990, although she was ninety-one, Helen's health was failing, but mentally she was as sharp as ever. I promised to visit her the following week, but unfortunately that was not to be. She died a few days later. I felt terribly sad and mourned her in my own way. A week later as a way to say my own goodbye and pay tribute in remembrance, I wrote my own recollection:

The phone call came that Sunday evening, and I was informed of Helen's death by a friend of her family. I accepted the news of my beloved friend's death with calm resignation. She was after all 91, and she had been in poor health for some time. The end was inevitable, I thought. I put aside the book I was reading when the call came, and I was suddenly overcome with a feeling of terrible sadness. I felt strangely alone once again. My aunt and I were close and I loved her, but Helen's relationship with me was on a different level. Memories of Helen flooded my thoughts.

Helen was not my mother, nor my aunt. She wasn't even a blood relative. To me, she was one of the unique people, who, in her sweet, unassuming way, became a beacon of everything that was right in this world. She genuinely and selflessly cared about people without reservation and without ever wanting something in return.

I had the unique privilege to meet Helen shortly after my arrival in New York from London in June of 1950 at the home of my great aunt, Mrs. Israel Davidson.

Over the many years since that June evening, Helen culti-vated our friendship. She became a trusted and caring friend.

Helen

She was the godmother to my older son. She gave me moral support when I needed it most, and instinctively, she felt my emotional needs. As though on cue, she would phone to find out how things were going.

Helen celebrated my accomplishments with quiet pride, and she was sympathetic and understanding when difficulties arose. She would often say, "you should never hesitate to call me; I think of you so often. I am your friend, and I care about you very much." She never missed my concerts, first the recitals in my teacher's studio and later those at Carnegie Recital Hall, Town Hall, and Philadelphia. She was supportive and happy for me when I decided to pursue formal academic studies. I was accepted at the University of Pennsylvania as a freshman, and then I continued my graduate studies at Temple University. She sent a dozen roses when I received my master's degree with a note saying, "I am so very proud of you. With all my love, Helen.' She was loyal, steadfast, and always encouraging.

Helen did many things for many people quietly, without fanfare or boasting about it. She genuinely liked helping people, and I know she extended a helping hand to many. She took an active interest in the things I was involved in. How fortunate I was in having her as my friend. She enriched my life with her tenderness and caring. She made me feel that somehow I too was part of her life.

Because I lived in Philadelphia and was busy pursuing academic degrees, while teaching at the same time, I could not visit Helen often. We used the phone as our means of communication. I would occasionally come to visit her in Mamaroneck, and we would spend many hours talking. She was always glad to see me, and she made me feel so welcome in her home. I relish those memories. She called me a few days before she went to the hospital for the last time. She sounded tired, and I didn't attribute that to any specific problem. In her usual gentle and non-complaining way, she told me that she wasn't feeling well a few weeks ago but was getting better. 'What can you expect at my age after all?' She never lost her keen sense of humor about herself.

Helen made a significant impact on my life, and she still fills a void in my life. She took an active interest in the life of my children, and she wanted to know everything about them. I have often cited her as an example of what is still good and righteous in this world. In a world where selfishness and greed are rampant, her gentle soul shone like a bright beacon for those of us who had the privilege to call her a friend. She was my angel.

She looked frail in the end, but this extraordinary woman who never raised her voice spoke very loudly. She never lost the strength of her convictions. I am deeply saddened and lonely knowing that I cannot pick up the phone and share with her my thoughts. Helen is no longer here, but I will recall most affectionately the memory of Helen Miller Davis who will live in my heart forever. She must be dwelling with the angels now...

One evening after a dinner party at Helen's apartment in the winter of 1950, shortly after I moved into my little room on Central Park West, I decided to walk home alone rather than be either escorted or driven, as was offered by one of Helen's guests. It was a lovely, snowy December evening and I felt the need to walk. I assured everyone that my apartment was not very far and the stroll would do me good. I was wearing one of those mutton lamb coats that, from afar, may have looked like a real beaver coat. I thought I was still living in London where it was safe to leave the door unlocked, and when walking alone in the evening, I experienced no fear.

Well, in 1950, I was rather naïve and still trusting of strangers on the street. That particular evening, an incident taught me that New York was not London.

Before I left Helen's apartment, I called my landlady to tell her that I had forgotten my key and asked if she could please buzz me in when I rang our bell in the entrance hall. I was walking leisurely toward my apartment when I was suddenly aware that I was being followed. At first, I didn't think much of it. By the time I entered the small lobby of our building and rang the bell waiting for the entry buzzer, the street door opened with a bang. A young man holding a switchblade in his hand pointed at my purse. I may have had a few dollars in my purse, and logically, I should have given him the money.

But something stirred in me, and without giving it much thought, I kicked him as hard as I could. He fell to the floor! Cursing in Spanish, I could see the anger in his eyes as he tried to get up from the floor. I realized that he had every intention to stab me to death!

Luckily, as though on cue, my landlady buzzed me in at that moment. I ran and slammed the door as hard as I could just as my attacker was trying to catch me. My landlady was elderly, and I did not want to upset her by telling her what had happened. When she opened the door to our apartment, she remarked that I looked a bit agitated. I told her as calmly as I could that I was fine and had just taken a long walk.

At that time I was dating a young man who was in for the weekend from Yale. He came to pick me up the next evening at my aunt's apartment, and I told them both what happened the night before. They could hardly believe that I did not call the police to report what could have been a major tragedy. My aunt immediately phoned the police and explained the situation. The police officer asked if I was there and asked to speak to me. First, he wanted to know if I could give him a description of the man. Then he said in a very calm but firm voice, "Young lady, you are either very foolish or extremely brave, and definitely very unusual. For your sake in the future, don't *ever* do that again. If someone holds a knife to you, give him your purse. I hope you will take my advice very seriously."

In retrospect, it was rather naïve of me to act so courageously, and it was probably very stupid. I simply felt indignant that someone could accost me and that I should do nothing about it. Without realizing it at that time, I simply fought back as a spontaneous response. Maybe I was learning how to function in the post-camp years. Nevertheless, that incident taught me to be more aware of my surroundings. My date could talk of nothing else that evening and said that he could not have responded that way. "You have remarkable courage, and I admire you for that," he said. In retrospect, I wasn't trying to be brave; it was probably very foolish, and I reacted to that incident without thinking of the consequences.

During my first year in New York, I was invited numerous times by various organizations to sing the *Star Spangled Banner* at opening ceremonies. I was thrilled to accept the invitation, and I started to feel that America was now *my* country too. I dutifully got the music and memorized all four verses; I also read the history behind our National Anthem. I only sang one verse though and received $25 every time I "performed".

A few weeks after I moved into my own room, I got a job working as a dental assistant, and then some time later, I was offered a job to be the office nurse to a distinguished surgeon. I was flattered that Dr. Rothenberg was willing to train me, particularly after I read his impressive credentials. His walls were covered with degrees and distinguished awards, among them he was Diplomat of the American Board of Surgery, Fellow of the American College of Surgeons, Civilian Consultant to the United States Army, Chairman of the Medical Group Council, and Member of the Board of Directors of the Health Insurance Plan of Greater New York. I assisted him in his Fifth Avenue office as well as in his Brooklyn Heights Center. Although my wages were modest, I was now independent and paying my own rent and expenses.

I found working for Dr. Rothenberg exciting, and it was a learning experience. He insisted that I accompany him on a few occasions to the operating room and observe surgical procedures. I was terrified and told him that I really didn't want to go, but he insisted by saying it would give me greater understanding of his patients' needs. I could hardly believe that I actually joined him for breakfast afterwards.

My parents would have never imagined that I chose to work in both dentists' and a doctors' offices *willingly*. As a child, I was absolutely terrified of dentists and doctors. I tried to analyze this, and I recognized later that rather than running away from something scary, I would jump right into it thereby overcoming the fear. I don't know how Freud would explain that. I asked Dr.

Rothenberg why he hired me over other much more qualified applicants. He said that he did not need a registered nurse for his office; instead he chose to train someone specifically for his office practice. "There were many more qualified applicants," he explained, "but although you had no experience, I recognized your willingness to learn, your innate intelligence, and your genuine interest about the job. You also have the right personality to be able to handle patients in stressful situations," he added.

I worked for him for three years, and he became a good friend. I would occasionally stay with his children when he and his wife went away for long weekends. In 1955, five years after arriving in the US and when I became eligible for American citizenship, he coached me for the test and stood as my witness. I was then married and eight months' pregnant. My eldest son Ronald was born a month later to an American mother!

While working for Dr. Rothenberg, I continued to study voice under Helen's scholarship. And I was also dating a number of men. There was one incident that was actually very funny. One of my friends from London invited me to dinner while visiting New York. I had dated his brother in London, and before I left for New York, he gave me a very attractive cigarette holder from Tiffany's as a gift. I smoked a little in those days, which made me feel very grown up.

While dining with my friend's brother in New York, I lost the cigarette holder his brother had given me. I don't know why, but he somehow felt responsible for my losing the holder. A few days later I received a letter with a gift certificate for $25 from Tiffany's to replace the holder. I thought it was totally unnecessary, but since he had already left for London, I decided to use it.

I had never been to Tiffany's and didn't know that it was one of the most beautiful and expensive jewelry stores in New York. A week later, I confidently entered that gorgeous store and walked over to the display window where exquisite necklaces and earrings were displayed. I thought I could get something different than a cigarette holder and in my naiveté, I thought I could buy a necklace or earrings with my gift certificate.

The elegant salesman was showing me two or three different necklaces and, looking at a particularly impressive one, I asked the price. I tried to keep my composure when he quoted the price, not of $25 but of $25,000! I apologized for wasting his time, explained my situation and the amount of my gift certificate. We both laughed and he politely directed me to the third floor where he suggested that I could buy very nice stationery for that amount. For the next year, I was writing my letters on Tiffany stationery. I am sure people were impressed!

In late 1953, I met Howard Harris. He was very handsome and personable, and I enjoyed being with him. He was very supportive of my musical talent, and he seemed to take pleasure when he occasionally accompanied me to my voice lessons and attended my student recitals. We started to date seriously.

One evening a few months later, he told me that he was planning a special party for mutual friends, and I thought that was great. When I came in that evening, I thought it was rather odd that he also invited his parents, his sister and brother-in-law, and other members of his family as well. Suddenly, people became very quiet, and while everyone was holding a drink, he knelt down and offered me an hors d'oeuvre. On top was a beautiful sparkling diamond engagement ring! I was totally taken by surprise. There was applause and congratulations from everyone when I said yes.

We originally set the date for June 1954. As we continued to date, I felt that I needed more time because I wasn't sure that we were right for each other. I started to get serious doubts. I knew we came from different backgrounds, but then, my background was different from everyone's! I was very fond of his mother and his sister, and his father was also very nice. They all made me feel that I would be very welcome in their family. It always amazed me then, as well as now, when people would meet, they would find that they either went to the same school or to the same summer camp or lived in the same neighborhood. I thought it was great, but I certainly felt somewhat out of place. Howard had many good qualities, and I loved him. I just wasn't

Nina and Howard Harris

sure that he was the right man for me. Nevertheless, I left my doubts behind; we were married in September 1954.

Our first son, Ronald, was born in September 1955, and our second son, Edward, followed in March 1958. I was thrilled to be a mother since I wasn't sure that I would be able to have children. While in Auschwitz, I worked for a while in the sterilization chamber and I didn't know if I might have been affected.

Over those ensuing years, my marriage to Howard just wasn't going anywhere and all the doubts I had before marriage were coming true. We were culturally miles apart. He was a nice Jewish boy from Brooklyn, and I was from another world. We tried to make it work, but I realized that there was no way I could continue to live with him. It was agonizing.

In the meantime, I continued to study voice and also take sessions with my vocal coach. My repertoire was expanding, and I eagerly looked forward to my weekly lessons. It gave me a needed intellectual outlet.

My teacher suggested that I should sign with a manager, and I did. The manager immediately auditioned me for the Philadelphia Grand Opera, and I was offered small roles in *Carmen, Suor Angelica,* and *La Rondine*; I sang with the company for two seasons. I traveled to Philadelphia, and at that time, I did not realize the significance Philadelphia would eventually have in my life.

In 1959 the situation with Howard came to a head, and I was determined to end our marriage. I simply could not continue to feel so lost and unhappy. Howard was a decent guy, but it became more and more apparent to me that we had different needs. I had to get on with my life and asked for a divorce. We were finally divorced in 1961. It was difficult. I had no money and no family, except for my aunt, and two very young children. My aunt was a career woman who had never married. She led a very busy life. She was a noted lecturer, the Director of Community Education and Field Activities, and the Director of the unique Rare Book Library of The Jewish Theological Seminary of America, a position from which she became known to most Conservative rabbis and most Jewish scholars in America.

Helen was very supportive of my decision. She was not thrilled when I married Howard, and she too had doubts about our union. Difficult as it was, I knew I had made the right decision. I was frightened and uncertain about how I would manage but deep down, I knew it was the right thing to do. Howard initially didn't want a divorce; he was hoping we would have more children, but he eventually realized there was no turning back.

When finally our marriage dissolved, I found a small, one-bedroom, rent-controlled apartment in Queens. I received very little financial help from Howard in the divorce settlement: eighty-nine dollars a week. I didn't care. I kept telling myself that somehow I would manage. I moved into my little apartment with the only two people who mattered to me in the whole world, Ronnie and Eddie. I gave them the bedroom, and I slept on the living room sofa bed. The children later understood that I divorced their father as much for their sake as for mine.

In 1964, I got a job with the National Cash Register Company (NCR) at the New York World's Fair. NCR had one of the three major exhibits and drew a great many people. I was originally hired to demonstrate banking machines, and I actually found it quite interesting. The demonstration essentially followed the steps of a check from the time it is first written through its "journey" or process, until it is returned to the depositor with the monthly statement.

I was all set to put my newly acquired "skill" to use when, a week before the Fair opened, management approached me. I was somewhat nervous, wondering what they wanted. "We have been watching you; we like the way you make the presentation and the way you handle yourself," they said. "The person we originally hired to demonstrate the main exhibit didn't work out, and we would like you to take over that exhibit." There was also a substantial raise in wages.

I had to memorize a twenty-eight page script that took twenty-five minutes to present to the public. The pavilion was very impressive. I walked around a large stage explaining each exhibit, starting with the old fashioned manual cash register. The exhibit pointed to the genealogy of the digital, electronic computer and how it led to the evolution of the more advanced computer age.

The management of NCR was pleased with my presentation and the public's response to the exhibit. At the conclusion of the Fair, they offered me a permanent job in the Public Relations department at its headquarters in Dayton, Ohio. The job description also included the responsibility of training people in public speaking presentations.

Prior to getting a job with NCR, I continued with my voice studies even though I recognized that unless I made a total commitment to a music career, I would get nowhere. My manager was furious with me. I would audition and get offered a part, but turned it down because I found it very difficult to travel and leave the children with strangers. My first and only commitment was to my children, and unless there were other means of caring for them, a serious career was out of the question.

I did accept a role singing with The Washington Opera Society, which was a very gratifying experience. The opera was *Carmen* and I was offered the part of Frasquita. It was performed in the original French with spoken dialogue. The opening performance was attended by a distinguished audience, including Jacqueline Kennedy. She was escorted by Conrad Adenauer, the Chancellor of Germany, since the President could not attend. There was a fabulous post-opera reception for the members of the cast at Decatur House hosted by Mrs. Kennedy.

The next morning, I found myself positively singled out above the leading cast with an impressive review by Washington's severe critic, Paul Hume. Nevertheless, I often felt insecure. I was essentially appearing with all professional singers who were totally committed to full careers and all of whom had degrees from the best music conservatories, including Julliard and Curtis. I, however, relied purely on my natural vocal and musical abilities. I had studied voice and repertoire, but the rest I did pretty much on my own. Memorizing music and languages came easily to me, and I had no difficulty mastering roles that were offered.

My teacher suggested that I audition for the Concert Artists' Guild and Town Hall competition, and I accepted. Requirements for the audition were quite rigorous. The prerequisite was to perform all or some of a complete vocal recital that had to include different languages and styles. My concert repertoire ranged from Monteverdi and German *Lieder*, to French and Russian songs, operatic arias, and songs by contemporary English and American composers.

Never thinking that I would have a chance to win, I was quite surprised when I was notified that out of over 150 entrants, encompassing both vocalists and instrumentalists, I was one of only six finalists. I shared the stage in Town Hall with a talented Korean pianist from the Julliard School of Music.

Soon after the concert I received a call from one of the Board Members of the Concert Artists' Guild, asking me if I was dating anyone seriously. I told her that I was dating, but I was not serious about him. For over a year I was involved in a great relationship with a gorgeous man whose company I enjoyed, but I knew that I was not going to marry him and expressed those sentiments to him shortly after we met.

When I asked the Board Member why she was interested in my romantic life, she told me about a "great guy" in Philadelphia, the nephew of one her friends, she enumerated his professional background: a master's from Harvard in Physics, the President of the International Foundation for Information Processing, the President of his own computer consulting firm, etc... He certainly sounded very impressive and according to her, he was of course the most eligible bachelor in Philadelphia. To some extent that might have been true.

It was also ironic that he was also linked with NCR, the company for which I was then working. He played an important part and was a pioneer in the original ground-breaking development of the legendary Eniac, the first electronic computer developed at the University of Pennsylvania. Isaac Auerbach was highly regarded in the world of computer science, and he was greatly respected for his innovative contributions. He also designed computer software for NCR.

Well, I said, "It all sounds very interesting. If you think he is also a nice person, you can give your friend, his aunt, my phone number." A few days later, I received a call from Isaac who asked if I could meet him at the Plaza Hotel for a drink two days later.

"Could we make it at seven o'clock because I have to catch a ten o'clock train back to Philadelphia?" he asked. I told him 7:30 would be more convenient because I had to arrange for a baby-sitter.

I walked into the Plaza Cocktail Lounge and scanned the room since I had no idea what he looked like. He spotted me, walked toward me, and introduced himself. He sounded very formal as he escorted me over to his table in the corner of the lounge. There seemed to have been an immediate *simpatico* reaction from both of us. He looked very dignified, and I liked his looks. I am not sure what he expected me to look like, but he kept looking at me with great interest; he hardly took his eyes off me. We ordered drinks and talked about each other, but he kept steering the conversation to me. He wanted to know everything about me.

I sensed that he was not always comfortable talking about himself. He told me that he was married for only two years; he had one son, Philip, and he had been divorced for over nine years. As the evening progressed, I felt that he was genuinely interested and fascinated with his blind date. Something was happening between us and since it was obvious that I was going to be home later than I thought, I called my baby-sitter and asked her to stay on.

There can be a moment when two people meet and a certain indefinable synergy penetrates the air around them. That is what happened between Isaac and me. I felt very attracted to him, and the feeling was obviously mutual. We had a lot to talk about when I finally stirred the conversation away from me to other subjects.

Isaac never took the ten o'clock train back to Philadelphia. He also didn't take the eleven o'clock train or the midnight train. I finally told him that I had to go home. We took a taxi to my apartment that at that hour was about twenty minutes from the Plaza. We obviously enjoyed each other's company and continued to converse. It was getting late into the night, and I finally suggested that he better get a train back to Philadelphia before I serve him breakfast! I called for a taxi to take him to Pennsylvania Station.

And so began a whirlwind six-month relationship that started in late April 1964. This was also the period when I was working at the World's Fair NCR pavilion and the management offered me a permanent PR job at the Dayton headquarters. I regretfully declined the job offer to re-settle in Dayton, Ohio, and I moved to Philadelphia, Pennsylvania instead. During the time we dated, Isaac came to see the exhibit, and I jokingly asked him how my presentation was. He said, "Well, now I know I have learned something!" I thought it was amusing, and we both laughed.

During the six months of courting, I was actually quite overwhelmed by Isaac's attention. He had to leave for Europe for four weeks the week after we met, and he said he would write. He was normally very reserved, and in the few postcards and two letters those qualities came across. He wrote how much he enjoyed meeting me and was looking forward to seeing me again.

I received a phone call from Philadelphia the evening he returned from Europe. A few days later, Isaac came to New York to see me. My World's Fair schedule was quite irregular with different shifts: some shifts were mornings, and others were afternoons and evenings. He would drive to New York on the days when I was not working. He would call almost every day, and he didn't hesitate to say how much he missed me.

One of Isaac's nicest qualities was his warmth and caring for my children. That really clinched it for me. My children came first. Their welfare was, and has always remained, my top priority. No matter how much I might have loved someone, if he were not good to my children, I would never have considered marriage.

Isaac and I spent many hours together in New York going to the best restaurants, boating on the lake in Central Park, and spending a few delightful weekends in a lovely country inn. He would send flowers with wonderful and romantic messages. He suggested that I come to Philadelphia for a weekend, and he thought it would be a good idea for me to meet his family. The relationship was obviously getting very serious.

I came to Philadelphia for a weekend, and I saw Isaac standing on the platform as the train pulled into the station. He greeted me warmly, and he was clearly happy to see me. I was a bit surprised that Isaac put me up in a hotel a block from his apartment. Perhaps he thought his family would consider it improper for "a young lady" to spend a weekend with him in his apartment.

The next afternoon he took me to meet his aunt. She reminded me of a *grande dame* and she used her stage name in normal life. I didn't know why Isaac felt so ill at ease but I noticed how uncomfortable he felt around her. There was something in her manner, that could have been construed as being intimidating, but it didn't phase me. I thought she was an elegant lady with an original personality. She was projecting airs about being an opera singer. She was clearly not royalty. She was a successful local voice teacher and appeared some years earlier in a few opera productions, but she was not known for her opera performances. She clearly explained to me in front of Isaac the first time I met her, "I had to give up my career to take care of the children when their parents died within six months of each other in 1936."

When we left her apartment, Isaac tried to explain the reason for the unusual closeness of his family. He was fourteen when he and his two younger sisters lost both parents. Isaac's unmarried aunt, then thirty-five, and her deceased brother (his unmarried uncle) brought the children up. There was no question that the children had been provided a good and caring home. But I can imagine how guilty and obligated he must have felt that his aunt had to "sacrifice" her career. In those days, if you did not have an active career at thirty-five, you were most likely not going to have one.

Isaac catered to his aunt, and I noticed how carefully he would construct his words when in her presence. He spoke to her as if to give me a signal that she was in control; one did not disagree with her or broach a subject that might be considered confrontational.

That evening we went to dinner with his sisters and their husbands. I felt that there was a false formality when we were introduced. Something stirred within me, a sort of warning sign. I found them cold and uninviting. Their husbands were friendly, but I felt that his sisters viewed me with suspicion.

I have always felt comfortable in any crowd, but there was something unnatural in their behavior. They tried to show how close the family was and how much they enjoyed being with each other. I thought they were putting on a show for my benefit. I felt uncomfortable, and Isaac recognized my apprehension. It wasn't necessarily me *per se*; they didn't know me. It was the first time we met and it didn't matter. He was their special brother, and perhaps they thought that no woman was good enough for him. As the dinner progressed, I noticed how tense he became. I had seen him before only away from Philadelphia, alone and in a different setting. I was surprised at the change in him. He held my hand as though to reassure me that all was well. Without realizing, he squeezed my hand so tightly that it hurt.

There was no question that I was deeply in love with him and, equally importantly, I regarded him with great respect. I had genuine feelings of unquestioned love for a man who so totally overwhelmed me with deep affection and reciprocal love. After dinner on the way back, he talked to me again about his family as if to reassure me that they were just not accustomed to seeing him obviously serious about me.

A few weeks later, on my second weekend in Philadelphia, we had a wonderful time. This time I stayed with him at his place. He had lived with his younger sister and her family for eight years after his divorce, and he had moved into his own apartment about two years before. I thought it was odd for a successful grown man (he was now 42) to have lived with his sister and her family for so long. It was obvious that he had a special place in her heart. Any woman would be considered a stranger and could never be anything else. His first wife and his son Philip were never really accepted into this tight web. His aunt was the matriarch of the family, and his sisters were equally possessive and controlling.

The following day we walked all over town, and he proudly showed me Philadelphia. We finally sat down on a bench in front of the Rodin Museum on the Parkway. He took my hands in his and pensively said, "I have been single for ten years since my divorce, and this is the first time I feel at peace with myself to ask you this question. My beloved, I am asking you to be my wife. Will you share your life with me?"

I was deeply touched with the way he phrased the proposal. There was nothing gushy about it, just deep and honest feelings, something I knew was not easy for him to express because he had difficulty showing his emotions. Isaac appeared rather stiff and formal whenever we would first meet, and then after a little while, he shed his tension and he would slowly unwind. He often said to me many times later and in his letters that I knew just how to put him at ease and make him feel relaxed and comfortable. I always felt that he was trying very hard not to show how tense he was, and I wondered what caused him such stress. Having met his family, I understood.

My third weekend in Philadelphia was very exciting. We met a few of his friends who made a big fuss over me. Isaac gave me a beautiful heart shaped brooch studded with little opals as an engagement present instead of the usual ring. Maybe because he was a Libra, he chose his birthstone. We also went shopping for a wedding ring, and we chose a band surrounded by little diamonds. Life looked so promising! I couldn't wait to come home and tell the children.

During our evening conversation he took out a document, and while holding it he said, "I am really concerned that just in case something should happen to me before we marry, I have taken out a $50,000 life insurance policy for you." I was puzzled and totally surprised at his generosity and thoughtfulness. I insisted that it was absolutely not necessary, and I wouldn't feel comfortable about it. I refused to sign it, but he insisted.

Years later, I was told that what he asked me to sign was a pre-nuptial agreement—without telling me that what I had signed had nothing to do with any insurance policy. I was shocked. It never occurred to me that he could be so under-handed! I would have been perfectly happy to sign a pre-nuptial agreement without the farce of calling it something it was not. I didn't know that there was such a thing as a pre-nuptial agree-ment, me, the eternal naive girl.

When I returned home from Philadelphia I called my aunt and described my weekend. I told her how happy I was, how wonderful Isaac was, and how great life was going to be when I move with the children to Philadelphia. "I love him very much, although there is something about his family I cannot under-stand and am not sure I like." She told me that I would be mar-rying Isaac and not his family. She was wrong. You marry Isaac; you marry his family. They came together as one total package.

Chapter 8

Philadelphia

On November 5, 1964, six months after we had first met, our wedding was held at his aunt's apartment with only the very immediate family present. His aunt even had reservations and mild objections to having my dear friend Helen who came from New York with my aunt Anita.

I traveled from New York that morning with Ronnie and Eddie, rightfully excited, and looking forward to my marriage to Isaac, what seemed like a promising and meaningful future.

When we arrived at her Locust Street apartment, what I did not expect to hear was the uncalled for and strange greeting with which his aunt "welcomed" me. "Well, well, my dear," she announced, "you know I am not making this wedding for you. I am doing it for Isaac!" I felt a knot in my stomach, and for a moment, the shock of that utterance left me stunned. I had hoped that the children didn't hear that selfish and self-centered remark.

My first reaction was to turn around and run the other way. What a dreadful thing to say! Perhaps Isaac should have a wedding without a bride? I was grateful that the rabbi welcomed me with a great big, bear hug embrace. I had met him only twice and liked him a lot. I think he understood the strange complex family structure of that family. When Isaac brought me to meet him a few weeks before our wedding, the rabbi told me how much he liked and highly respected my aunt Anita, who was known to every conservative rabbi who ever studied at The Jewish Theological Seminary of America…

My aunt, Anna Kleban (the family called her Anita), was the Director of Community Education and Field Activities of the Library of the Jewish Theological Seminary of America. She also had the responsibility of guiding visitors through the treasures of the Rare Book Room, the only such library of Jewish learning in the world.

Anita devoted her life to the Rare Book Library where she worked for fifty-six years, and over the decades, she had the opportunity to work with some of the world's greatest Jewish scholars. Her talks were interlaced with humor and anecdotes, delighting her audience and bringing medieval manuscripts to life. With a rare combination of knowledge, remarkable wit, charm, and her love of books, she enchanted audiences of all ages and ranks. When I would hear one of her presentations and get a personal tour (I had clout), she would say, "Where else can you find history all in one case, a veritable United Nations of precious items: a Bible from Egypt, a prayer book from Germany, a Megillah from Persia, a Haggadah from Spain, a marriage contract from Greece, a medical book from Italy, and a book on algebra, written in Yiddish, from Poland?"

She was a noted lecturer and greatly in demand throughout the country to share her knowledge with many audiences. She was well known to scholars and librarians all over the world. She invented a lecture series called "Behind the Parchment Curtain", and people were mesmerized listening to her stories of the tales of Jewish books and how they found their way to the Seminary Library. What made her lectures quite special was partially due to her personal touch and keen sense of humor. Her wealth of knowledge and early interest in books came through her background (my background as well.) Her father, my grandfather, was a noted Hebraist, cantor, and rabbi in Grodno. Her uncle, my great uncle, Professor Israel Davidson, was one of the foremost authorities on medieval Jewish poetry and literature.

Anita had a strong knowledge of five languages and spoke all quite well. Sadly, Isaac's aunt and sisters were not interested in knowing much about my family. I hardly ever talked about them.

On our wedding day, Isaac's son Philip, age eleven, showed a sincere sense of excitement. He was charming, sweet, and attentive; I was very impressed with him. He greeted me warmly and was delighted to take over the responsibility of being the genial host to my boys, then ages nine and six and a half. Present were Isaac's two sisters, their husbands and their children. The affection with which Isaac treated my children and his obvious love for me made up for everything. I was completely devoted to Isaac and Philip and to the prospect of a wonderful marriage.

The wedding ceremony was meaningful, and, in spite of the discomfort I felt at the beginning, all went smoothly. We spent our delightful four-day honeymoon in a lovely and secluded inn in Connecticut. We separated for a few days; I returned to New York and Isaac returned to Philadelphia, and two days later we left from New York on a wonderful ten-day trip to Europe.

At that time, Isaac was the President of the International Federation of Information Processing (IFIP). We combined our honeymoon with his responsibilities as President of the International Federation. We first spent a few exciting days in Amsterdam; then we went on to Rome where Isaac was chairing a conference. I was warmly welcomed and embraced by his international colleagues, who paid a great deal of attention to me. After Italy, we flew to Zurich where Isaac had scheduled to meet a business friend. When we arrived at our hotel, the magnificent Bauer au Lac, a dozen exquisite yellow roses were waiting for me in our room. For dinner that evening we were to meet Isaac's friend, a banker with whom Isaac had some business dealings. What I did not expect was to meet this strikingly attractive debonair and elegant gentleman, Uli, who warmly welcomed us to Zurich.

During a long and enjoyable dinner, the topic of conversation eventually turned to art, and he was pleasantly surprised when I said that I liked the paintings of Paul Klee. "Why don't we go to my office after dinner and you can see a few of his paintings? I am a great admirer of his," he suggested. The walls of Uli's impressive office suite were covered with paintings, obviously all originals.

Taking my hand, he proceeded to tell us the history of each painting and particularly those of Klee. There was no doubt that his attention was focused on me and not on Isaac. I was flattered but felt uncomfortable about that. After all, I was on my honeymoon! There, somehow, developed a strong attraction between us. It simply just happened.

When we left his office, he kissed my hand, then turned to Isaac, and said, "You are lucky. Your wife is charming and a very beautiful woman." Isaac mentioned this to me when we returned to our hotel, and of course, I dismissed it for what it was, an unexpected moment of *simpatico.*

A few days later, we were invited to Uli's home to join him and his wife for dinner, although I was told that this is normally not customary. He sent a driver to pick us up, and we spent a wonderful evening in the magnificent surroundings overlooking Lake Lucerne. His wife was a gracious hostess, and although we were only a small group of four, three servants catered to us. I felt an unmistakable synergy drawn between Uli and me, and I felt his presence very strongly. I was in love with my new husband, and I couldn't understand my own sudden, confusing feelings toward this fascinating man. Before we left Zurich, Uli presented us with a parting gift: a beautifully illustrated book of art from the Museum of Fine Arts, Basel (Kunstmuseum Basel) that included photographs of six Paul Klee paintings. When I opened it, the inscription read: "To remember an evening spent in a spirit of warm friendship… and anxious to spend many more hours together". Our names were not part of the inscription. Our eyes met, and he handed the book to me. I met him only once more in New York some years later, and he told me that he and his wife were divorced.

We returned home from Europe after our honeymoon. Isaac held my hand practically all the way back to New York and told me what a positive impression I had made on his colleagues. A few days after I came home, I moved to Philadelphia. Ours was a lovely, spacious apartment, close to the house of Isaac's son Philip, who lived with his mother and stepfather. Philip was with us as often as possible, which was basically every weekend. Ronnie and Eddie started school, adjusted very well to their new life, and I was very grateful that Isaac was good to them. Some months later, they started calling him Dad, (at their suggestion) in spite of the mild objection from their father. Every few weeks, I put them on a bus to New York so that they could spend a weekend with their father.

Life was good. There were no problems except for the tension I felt in Isaac toward his family. I was beginning to feel that maybe I was doing something wrong, and I confronted him about it. He dismissed it out of hand and said that they simply were very close knit, they had to get used to a "stranger". For a man who lived in Philadelphia all his life, I was surprised that Isaac had no close friends. I thought it was odd. He knew many people, of course, and was respected in his profession, but these people were acquaintances with whom we socialized. I traveled to New York occasionally to continue my studies with my vocal coach. And I was also fortunate to find a very fine pianist locally, who became my accompanist. We would spend an hour or so a week so I could continue to add to my repertoire. I was aware of course that Isaac was not particularly interested in my career, and I was not interested in having one. I just loved singing. And he enjoyed my singing—as long as I was doing it for fun.

Two years after I had moved to Philadelphia, I was asked by one of our friends to give a concert in their spacious and beautiful Haverford home. My accompanist, Gertrude Flor, and I prepared a full vocal recital consisting of different styles in five languages; it was received with great enthusiasm. Unbeknownst to me, they invited Sol Schoenbach, the Director of the

Settlement Music School.

Settlement was, and is, an old and established music school that was, in fact, the start of the Curtis Institute of Music, one of the finest conservatories in the country. After the concert, Sol approached me and asked me if I would be interested in joining the vocal faculty at Settlement. He also asked if I would send my curriculum vitae. I told him that I had an extensive vitae, but no formal degrees of any kind, musical or otherwise. His answer to me was very welcome. "What you have and what you can do with a student a degree cannot give you. Our school would be very happy to add your name to our voice faculty."

And so I began my teaching career with Settlement; I taught there for over twelve years. I was also asked to join the board of the Alumni and Friends of the School. The purpose was to present three or four concerts a year, each featuring world-class artists. The money from the concerts was given to the school for its scholarship funds. During those years, I gave many fundraising benefit concerts for various organizations around Philadelphia. I also occasionally accepted an invitation and sang the soprano lead for a special concert. I particularly enjoyed singing with the New Jersey Symphony Orchestra in Bruckner's *Te Deum*. I don't think my husband enjoyed traveling with me on those occasions. In other words, he did not want me to sing professionally, and I had to emphasize that giving a fundraising concert was beneficial for the community.

One day when I came to school, I found a note from Sol Schoenbach telling me that Leopold Stokowski was going to conduct the Philadelphia Orchestra for the benefit of the Orchestra's Pension Fund. (Sol was first bassoonist with the Philadelphia Orchestra for twenty-five years under Stokowski; he was a highly regarded musician.) At that time Stokowski was also the conductor of his own Orchestra in New York, and they performed at Carnegie Hall.

Sol informed me that Stokowski was interested in performing an unknown Russian aria from a rarely heard Tchaikovsky opera. Sol gave me the name of the aria; he told me that

Stokowski wanted to hear me after the rehearsal while he was in Philadelphia to conduct the Pension Fund concert. It was a rather long and difficult piece of music, but I had no difficulties singing it. The range with the high Cs felt comfortable in my voice and came easily to me. I learned the aria and told Sol that I would be honored to sing for the great maestro.

A few days later, Sol received a letter from Stokowski apologizing that he did not have enough time before he left for New York to hear me in Philadelphia. "Would Miss Kaleska consider coming to New York to sing for me?" Well yes, Miss Kaleska certainly would be happy to come to New York to sing for the maestro! The following week, my accompanist Gertrude Flor, Sol, and I traveled to New York for my audition. I was well prepared with four major arias, including the seldom performed Russian aria he wanted to hear. I entered his Fifth Avenue apartment, nervous but excited. He was, after all, a legend in his own time.

Stokowski greeted us warmly. Sol warned me that Stokowski didn't always hear the entire piece during an audition; I should not get upset if I got to sing only for five minutes. It was fascinating the way Stokowski "orchestrated" the audition. He wanted me to stand at a certain spot in front of the piano, and Sol was to sit at another part of the studio while he sat at his desk near the window overlooking Central Park. I had the privilege to sing for him for twenty-two minutes!

It certainly turned out to be a very interesting audition. I not only sang the prepared work, but he asked me to sing other arias as well. I sang Mozart and Prokofiev. While I was singing, he kept writing at his desk. I was wondering if he was listening to me (yes, he was!). At one point he left the studio when he was called away for a phone call, and Sol said to my accompanist "Boy, would I love to read what he wrote, but I don't have my glasses." Gertrude looked at him and said, "I don't need glasses. You want me to peek?" I still remember the look on Sol's face when Gertrude whispered to him "glorious top, magnificent bottom", and with his sense of humor, Sol remarked, "Is he talking about her voice?"

Stokowski asked me to learn *Carmina Burana* and to come and sing for him again the following week. I learned *Carmina* and did not like the way the high note (high D) sounded in my voice. I called Leila Edwards, my coach in New York with whom I studied for many years, and told her that I didn't think I should sing *Carmina* because I wasn't comfortable with it.

Her answer was, "You silly goose, when Stoky was planning to perform *Carmina* the first time in New York in 1953, he auditioned every damned soprano in New York! Everyone had trouble with that particular passage, and I think you should definitely accept the opportunity to sing for him. He doesn't offer it to many singers."

But as far as I was concerned, either one has a natural and comfortable high D, such as a *bona fide* coloratura soprano, or not. I was a lyric soprano with strong high notes and a two and a half octave range, but a high D was not comfortable in my voice, particularly not in that passage. I kept thinking about it. This after all was Leopold Stokowski, New York, and Carnegie Hall. I was in Philadelphia getting no support from my husband. I told Sol that certain parts of the vocal line did not feel comfortable in my voice, and I didn't want to take a chance singing it. Sol was great and agreed with my feelings. He said that Stoky didn't conduct everything either, not if he didn't feel he could do full justice to it. (I couldn't imagine Stokowski not doing full justice to anything he conducted. He was absolutely the greatest.)

I wrote a letter to Stokowski expressing my great appreciation for the opportunity to sing for him, but I told him the *Carmina Burana* did not feel right for me. I also expressed the hope that in the future I would have the honor to work with him. When the season with his orchestra ended, he left for England. He died there a year later. He was eighty-six when I met him, but he was young at heart, exciting to be with, vigorous, and totally in charge. When I heard the news of his death, I felt sad, but I was grateful for the opportunity to have met him and sing for him.

In October of 1974, I was asked to present a concert at the Walnut Street Theatre in Philadelphia for the benefit of the Scholarship Fund of the Alumni and Friends of the Settlement Music School. I was the first faculty member to be asked to give a concert for the Alumni and Friends. It was also the first time that the school presented a concert at the historic Walnut Street Theatre. Prior to this, concerts had always been, and are still, held at the School Auditorium in its South Philadelphia branch. This concert had a standing room only audience and generated over $15,000 for the scholarship fund. It was a great success with the audience as well as the critics. After the concert, an elegant reception was planned in my honor in the beautiful Main Line home of our friends. People remarked to me later that after the concert when they congratulated Isaac about me in glowing terms, his response was ice cold.

I was not prepared for the comment Isaac made to me over the phone when he called from his of office the next day. I had not seen the reviews in the papers, and I was glad to hear from him. But I did not expect the frozen and almost resentful reaction to my success. "Did you see the reviews today? Well, the Metropolitan Opera is now waiting for you. This was your dream all along, wasn't it?"

I was deeply hurt to hear his comment. "No, I gave a concert for the benefit of the Settlement Music School; I worked very hard with little support from you. We will contribute over $15,000 dollars to the scholarship fund of the school, and I am very pleased that the concert generated such a full house and many contributions given to the school in my name. I would have thought you would have been proud of me and celebrated my success. What a pity that you cannot share my success as I share yours when you are honored. If I wanted to continue an active career and aspired to the Met, which as you know was never my intention, I would not have married you and moved to Philadelphia."

The reviews in *The Philadelphia Inquirer* and *The Evening*

Bulletin were very complementary. The caption in *The Bulletin* read: "Kaleska a Study in Serene Strength." In the lengthy description of the concert, it said:

"Vocally and dramatically versatile, she radiated a rare stage presence, a type which can only come from someone whose involvement with her art goes beyond competence and experience. Kaleska is gifted with a full, misty voice which changes registers effortlessly and can convey a myriad of moods. Her mastery brings each work to life in a way which makes scenery, costumes and other dramatic trappings seem like an intrusion...."

I felt that I had to apologize for being a success. How sad! I had no designs for a career; I enjoyed using my talent in a positive way that gave me an intellectual outlet by continuing to study languages and music. It would have been nice to have the support of my husband, who should have been proud and celebrated my accomplishments. I presented a concert that generated an 1,100-person standing-room-only house, great reviews, and thirty-five bouquets of flowers. Instead, I was made me to feel apologetic. I could not understand his resentment at my success. I was puzzled, and so was everyone else.

Chapter 9

Another Abyss

A few weeks after my acclaimed concert at the Walnut Street Theatre, I was still receiving letters of congratulations. I taught one day a week, always on a Wednesday, and that evening when I came home from school and was preparing dinner for us, the conversation was directed to the activities of the boys and general topics. There was no indication that something rather drastic was about to happen.

After dinner when I was getting ready to go to bed, Isaac knocked at our bedroom door and said in his usual formal way, "May I talk to you for a moment?"

"Well of course, why the formality?"

His words still ring in my head. "Look, I don't know who I am. I am not happy; you are not worth loving; you are successful and admired; and you can cope on your own." I could hardly believe what he was saying. There was absolutely no indication that his feelings about our marriage had changed so drastically. The conversation at the dinner table was perfectly normal. There wasn't the slightest indication that a bombshell was about to fall.

I knew that he had difficulty coping with compliments about me (why, I never understood). I never felt anything but total devotion in my responsibilities as a wife and mother. A career was the last thing on my mind. I longed for a solid family relationship, and that meant everything to me. I thought I had that.

I looked at him dumbfounded, and frankly, I didn't know what to say. I suggested that this was not the way problems were solved, but with Isaac, a give and take conversation was not always possible. He decided what and when, and that was it. Perhaps he was not ready for my answer but I suggested that if he was so unhappy and he didn't know "who he was" (I never understood that expression), he should find out and then proceed with a divorce if that would make him happy. Perhaps he thought I would cry and plead. As shocked and devastated as I was, I knew that I would have to cope and, once again, make the best of a difficult situation that came as a shock to me. I wasn't sure how and when, but I would not stoop to melodrama. I left our bedroom and, deeply troubled, spent the night in the guestroom feeling rejected and puzzled.

Three weeks after the fateful "announcement", I came home from school, and as I approached our home, I noticed a strange configuration in the distribution of the lights in the house. All day at school, I had a strange sinking feeling in my stomach and wasn't sure why. The receptionist told me that someone had called twice to inquire if I was at school. She offered to call me to the phone, but the caller had said that it was not necessary. "What time is Nina's last student?" I thought it was an odd question, but I didn't pay much attention to it.

My premonition that day that something horrible was about to happen proved right. As I approached the driveway, I knew that something was terribly wrong. The ominous feeling I had all day had now totally engulfed me, but I still didn't know what it was. Why was the lighting in our dining room and living room dim? I parked my car in the garage and found Isaac's space empty. That was not so unusual, although he had told me in the morning that he would be home for dinner.

I walked in through the garage door to the kitchen, and slowly, moving from room to room, I was absolutely horrified to find that well over half of the house contents were gone... furniture, beds, blankets, pillows, paintings, rugs, dishes, cutlery, and more. It was disconcerting to find a headboard for two beds with one bed removed! It felt as thought one leg was amputated. He essentially left what I had brought with me from New York just over ten years earlier plus some furniture and rugs that could not fit in his new abode. I was dealing with a man who I found out later was very wealthy; he could have easily afforded to buy what he needed to set up his newly rented apartment without destroying and mutilating a household where my sons and I lived. His action appeared unconscionable. A few days later, I bought additional kitchen equipment and cutlery.

My son Eddie, who was sixteen and in eleventh grade, was in his room. I tried to wipe the shock from my face and knocked at his door. He was at his desk studying, or perhaps trying to study as I entered his room. I gently embraced him and then sat down on his bed. At first, I did not say anything. I was very concerned about the impact and emotional reaction the horrible action of someone we trusted had on him. Ronnie was already in his sophomore year at college and lived away on campus.

"Would you like to tell me how you feel and if you are alright? I think it would be helpful if you could tell me what happened. Were you home when all this was going on?" Eddie was amazingly calm but obviously very upset. He told me when the bus dropped him off in front of our house from school and he saw a large moving truck in front of our house, he didn't know what was going on. "My heart sank" was his response.

My own shock about the situation was justified. Isaac must have made a detailed list of all the things he wanted weeks before with the help of his efficient secretary, who, I was sure, reluctantly agreed to aid him. He planned everything very carefully. He never did anything spontaneously, and he was always in control. The sad part of it is he could have taken anything he wanted by just asking for it. He didn't have to stoop to acting like a thief in the night behind my back.

I reassured Eddie that things would work out. Material things could be replaced, but a reputation and trust had to be earned. Isaac stooped to a pretty low level with his ugly tactic, probably with the help of his attorney, who most likely gave him very bad advice. You have to know with whom you deal.

As a child, I had already lost everything…my family, my home, and material things. When I walked into my Philadelphia house many lifetimes later, I experienced a feeling of total dread; I was momentarily back in Auschwitz, and my body inadvertently shivered. I thought I had a home and security. Once again, I was left with doubt and uncertainty. It was more painful to experience such a deliberate, meaningless action. I blamed myself to some extent for having been so blind and trustful by thinking that this man who portrayed himself as a "pillar" of morality in the community, but fell into a such a deep chasm.

My only thought was for the well-being of my children. Eddie and I spent a while talking things out, and I was astonished at his strength and resilience. He was actually comforting me! I think he stopped being sixteen at this moment, and he became a young man of remarkable understanding. I didn't want to call Ronnie yet. I needed to digest the bizarre situation. I did call a neighbor, a well-known psychiatrist whose advice I appreciated when Isaac had confronted me a few weeks before. He knew Isaac and had attended my concert. He had predicted difficult days ahead. "He may take out his long, pent up frustrations stemming from many years ago on you because you are at the right place at the right time. He can't touch his family. His secretary wouldn't stand for it. That leaves you. He could not control you. Don't be surprised, and be ready for unexpected behavior."

Well, his analysis proved painfully correct. "Something has happened. Could you please come over? I really need you," I asked. He in turn inquired who was in the house, and I told him just Eddie and I.

He came over, and I told him what had happened. He looked around at the half empty rooms and said, "I want you to

put your head on my shoulders and cry. Let your emotions out."
No, I said, that's not my style. Crying is not going to help now.
I don't want Eddie to see me cry; I must be strong for the boys.
I will cry later, alone.

In May of that year, Isaac's letters from Japan expressed such
conflicting messages. "You have made me happier than I had
ever thought possible. I miss you terribly and can't wait to
embrace you." Then he wrote from Hong Kong, "My darling
wife… to go back to our phone call that was fantastically clear…
It was absolutely wonderful hearing your voice and your excitement and learning that all is going well at home… I long to be
home and sit next to you in the pool … Am anxious to hold you
and kiss you… I can't wait to see you… All my love."

That summer we had traveled to Europe and took Eddie
with us. Isaac was conducting a meeting for IFIP and once
again, his international colleagues made me feel very welcome.
We were in Sweden and were going on to Jerusalem where he
was to meet with the Director of Boys Town, for which he created a computer system.

Throughout Denmark and Sweden, I found Isaac extremely
tense and detached. I tried to speak to him about it, but communication was not his forte. It was difficult for him to share
feelings. When I asked what was bothering him—or perhaps it
was something I had said—he would just ignore it. Finally, I
suggested that since he was so involved with his work and I had
a concert to prepare, perhaps I should go home. "Absolutely
not," he said. 'We will go to Israel next week." And that was
that. He held my passport, and it was not convenient for him to
see me go alone. He made the decisions, and I had to abide.

After his abrupt departure when I met some of the people
who worked for him, I got a very disturbing picture of his
behavior. His employees viewed him as a dictator. He would
hire a highly qualified executive and then proceed to tell him
how to execute his job. Consequently, many top people

resigned. Isaac's son Philip, who worked at his company at the time, observed that Isaac would also deliberately create problems so that he could berate others and appear indispensable in solving them.

The same was true of the civic organizations where he served as a member of the Board. He would initiate a good plan, but then it had to be done his way or not at all. I once asked the elected president of one of the Jewish organizations on whose Board Isaac served why he was not elected president. I thought he was certainly very qualified. The answer was direct and blunt. "If Isaac were elected president, he would have to run the organization without a Board. People do not appreciate his attitude, and many would most likely resign. I am sure you must not have had an easy time being married to him." I knew how difficult he was, but I did not know how others felt about him. I was very saddened to hear so many negative comments about someone I once loved deeply and respected greatly.

The days and weeks following my shock at his actions were very difficult. While I functioned well on the outside, I felt a need to speak to someone about the pain and disappointment. A friend suggested that I speak with a professional. She made an appointment with a highly regarded psychologist, and the following day I spent two hours with her expressing my feelings. I blamed myself for not seeing him the way he was. I believed him, I suppose, because I wanted to. She looked at me at one point and said plainly, "Nina, difficult as it is for me to say this to you, you married one of your former oppressors. I know it sounds rather harsh, but he has all the markings of a cruel and dictatorial man. There is a lot of unresolved conflict within him, and you happened to be in the right place at the right time for him to unleash his frustrations on you." It was the same analysis as my psychiatrist friend!

Those words proved very true. Yes, the actions he took after he left the house were indeed cruel and so totally needless. I never knew how wealthy he was, and I never bothered to find out. I was really stupid and naïve. Material things were not important to me. I owed a department store $3.85 when we separated. I was always very careful how I spent my allowance. It was more important that he was kind to my children. Isaac was very cunning, never really trusted anyone, and left me with very little until we actually had to go to court! It was unthinkable.

When he asked me to sign our joint income tax, he would put his hand over the bottom line so that I would not see the final sum. When I think about it now, I know I was trusting, but that is my nature. There was no reason for me not to have trusted him. I loved him and had full confidence in him; I never imagined that the prince I thought I married would turn into an ugly frog. He left me with nothing. *He* was no longer in the house. Therefore *I* didn't need anything, right?

After Isaac left, I would receive $50 a week. He paid the household expenses. After almost two years of indecision on his part when he would come "home" on the pretence of seeing our dog, the masquerade was complete. I asked him please to bring the situation to a final conclusion and not to come to the house any longer. I couldn't stand living there, and I wanted to start my life anew, away from the tension of coping with the situation he had brought about. Apparently he wasn't quite ready for the final divorce. He was still testing his relationship with the woman who became his third wife. (My lawyer told me at the beginning that if he didn't get involved with someone else, it would be difficult to get a divorce.) I told him again and again that if he wanted a divorce, all he had to do was ask.

Acting like a thief and carefully planning to remove material possessions from our house, (I thought it was my house too, but apparently he did not) in such an uncivilized and degrading manner for a man of Isaac's stature, was revolting. I did not stand in his way. I could never live with a man who would stoop so low. I wanted out. Finally, it was my older son Ronnie who urged him to get things moving.

When I married him, I gave him all my life's savings, all of $8,000! He suggested that we invest it, and I thought it was a good idea. When time came for me to look at my financial situation, I asked him what he did with the money I gave him to invest. He said he didn't know, and it was probably invested with everything else. I called his investment broker and his accountant. They both had no knowledge of this transaction. I found out later that he invested it in his own name only.

To get any kind of settlement we had to go to court. The judge was stunned that a man of his stature acted in such a degrading manner. During the hearing, my esteemed husband suggested to the judge that I could easily earn my own living by giving concerts and giving lectures about the Holocaust! The judge emphasized that at age forty-five I was not about to embark on a singing career and that talking about my past to earn a living was a cruel suggestion. I had never accepted money when I was invited to participate in a symposium or civic organizations, except for receiving a customary small honorarium. I would speak to many high schools, college, and universities, always at a cost to me—emotionally. I was deeply wounded by those horrid remarks.

I left the courtroom quite shaken. Isaac approached me after the hearing in front of the courthouse. I looked at him, and calmly, in a quiet but determined voice, I said, "I have just excommunicated you from the Jewish faith. Don't ever call yourself a Jew in my presence again. If you have any conscience at all, think about your pitiful performance when even the judge was appalled at your suggestions. You and your esteemed lawyer have just stooped to a pretty low level." I don't know if my words had touched him, but he might possibly have thought about the course he decided to take when there was absolutely no need for such uncalled for action. I have never understood what compelled my husband to resort to such strange and unnecessary behavior toward me. I was deeply hurt and wronged, but time does heal. Holding ill feelings makes me uncomfortable, and I have forgiven him.

During the time of my separation, I became productive and busy. Life was difficult. I smiled on the outside and cried at night alone. I was angry with myself for being so naive and trusting. I should have recognized the many lies I was fed.

Soon after my divorce became final, I found a lovely small townhouse in center city Philadelphia, and I increased my teaching schedule. l continued singing with my accompanist and added new repertoire, purely for my own pleasure. I gave a few benefit concerts for various worthwhile organizations. I dated a few men, but my heart was not into a lasting relationship at that point. I had first to re-build my life once again and to become independent. I had more students than I could handle. I taught students at the Settlement Music School; students from the University of Pennsylvania, from Bryn Mawr and Haverford Colleges; and also private students. I was getting requests to speak at different conferences, to different schools and colleges; I would occasionally accept the invitations.

I was sitting at my desk one evening trying to gather thoughts in preparation for a talk I was invited to present at an Episcopal Church when a ring of laughter came across through the open windows in steady staccato tones. The night air brought with it a gentle breeze after a hot, oppressive day. The curtains waved gently flooding the room with the scent of the aroma emanating from the Wisteria bushes just under my bedroom window. The grand, old Japanese tree covered with magnolia flowers came to full bloom and looked beautifully illuminated by the light shining on it from my second floor porch. For two weeks every spring, nature graced the old tree with white splendor.

It was difficult to believe that my house was in downtown Philadelphia. It was so peaceful in my little garden, full of flowers and a tree. Someone once said that it looked like a page from *House Beautiful*. That evening only the laughter indicated that my little house was surrounded by neighbors. I was immersed in deep thoughts when the long awaited rain finally came, unleashing with it the furor of nature's wonders.

The heavens opened up, and it looked for a while as if the torrential waters would never cease. I opened the door to the garden and walked out, standing there, half-naked being soaked up by the warm shower of the downpour. I brushed my hair bending my face backward, thoroughly enjoying the feeling of being totally drenched. I suddenly remembered the time when my sister gathered rainwater into a bucket and washed her beautiful thick hair with it. I felt totally invigorated.

The worries of the days vanished, washed away with the flood from heaven. It had been a hard day, but somehow at that moment, it didn't matter. I walked back into the house not concerned that I dripped water all over the floor. I headed directly for the bathroom and took a long, warm shower. I finished preparing my talk, and the following evening I met my friend, a Jesuit priest, who asked me to join him for an ecumenical gathering. I thought it was significant when he introduced me by saying: "We have come a long way when a Jesuit priest introduces a Jewish woman to an Episcopal congregation." I thought so too!

In 1980 I accepted a position with The Philadelphia Singers, a sixteen-voice professional ensemble, one of a few professional choruses in the country led by its founder, director, and conductor Michael Korn. I met the charismatic and brilliant Michael Korn when he was looking for a public relations person. We hit it off immediately. He told me what the Singers organization needed to generate a greater audience, and I gave him ideas that he thought were exactly what he had in mind.

The Board of Trustees approved my joining the staff, and my successful association with the Singers, and particularly with Michael who became a close and trusted friend, lasted until he sadly and prematurely died of AIDS a few years later. Michael was also the Chorus Master for the Opera Company of Philadelphia. I admired his remarkable musicianship and appreciated his sharp sense of humor. I spent many enjoyable evenings at his home with his musician friends. I wrote and recorded a commercial for a number of local radio stations to promote Handel's *Messiah*, which The Philadelphia Singers performed for the first time at the Academy of Music. That performance sold out, and the Singers have continued to perform the *Messiah* there every Christmas season. The last year when Michael knew how far his AIDS had progressed, I became his confidant, and he would call me almost every evening to talk about many subjects. I was privileged to know him.

At that point, I decided that it was time to get a job that would generate more money than my teaching. Well, get a job; that's just fine. I had no qualifications for any specific job. Get real, Nina. Better find a way to get a different profession. I was convinced that I must get a formal education. One of my students suggested that I apply to the University of Pennsylvania. "Really," I said, "I don't even have a high school diploma!" Still, I was encouraged to pursue the idea of getting a college education.

I arranged an appointment with a councilor at the College of General Studies at the University of Pennsylvania. I got my dossier together, and I was quite surprised how much I had actually accomplished without the benefit of formal schooling. The only college units I had were from Queens College in New York when I took an extensive opera workshop for which I received two credits in music.

I approached the university for my interview with great apprehension. At age fifty-one, I had my dossier and a seventh-grade level schooling. It required courage to assume that I could be accepted and be ready to embark on a college education at this stage of my life without ever having formally studied English! The interview went well, and I was informed that judging by my life's accomplishments in various educational endeavors, I could be accepted as a student at the College of General Studies. "All we need is your high school diploma," I was told. Really, I thought. My high school diploma? I didn't even finish my junior high school! Nevertheless, I was profoundly pleased that I would even be considered for acceptance to the University.

The following day I called the School District of Philadelphia to find out what was necessary to go about getting the necessary information to obtain a General Education Diploma, a GED. I was advised to purchase the specific testing book that held the tons of information covering all the subjects that I would need to study to prepare for the final five-point test. The question the GED people asked me was: "In what grade did you drop out of high school, eleventh or twelfth?" I didn't answer. I just chuckled under my breath!

I needed a B or better for admission to Penn. I proudly purchased the heavy tome with full determination to study my tail off. For six weeks all I did, when I was not teaching, was study and try to absorb 500 pages of information, all of which was essentially new to me. English and Social Studies were no problem, but I had never studied high school Math or different parts of Science. I was concerned and scared. Luckily, one of my students, who had just graduated from the University of Pennsylvania Medical School, helped me understand the math and the science studies. I told her we could start with two and two make four, and then we could take it from there!

With great apprehension I bravely entered the assigned school where the GED tests were held. It seemed that I was the only "adult"; the students were mostly young, African American, high school kids. In a matter of ten days, I took the five different tests dealing with the high school subjects; I waited patiently for the final results. A few weeks later, I was relieved to learn that I successfully passed all five tests. I was now ready to write my letter of purpose—me, the high school graduate applying formally to the University of Pennsylvania!

Friends gave me a lovely "high school graduation" party. Among the many gifts and congratulations, I received a beautiful orchid from a friend whom I was dating at that time. He pinned it on my dress saying, "It is a long-standing tradition that a high school graduate gets to wear an orchid, so you shall have one too." The whole affair was really quite touching.

Chapter 10

Academia

That evening I started to carefully compose my Letter of Purpose addressed to the University of Pennsylvania Faculty of Arts and Sciences, College of General Studies:

October 22, 1980

You have requested a statement of purpose about my academic and personal background and information about my non-academic experiences that will strengthen my application for admission to the University of Pennsylvania, College of General Studies.

I was born in Grodno, Poland in 1929. In June 1939, Poland was divided between the Soviet Union and Germany. Grodno became part of the Soviet Union from 1939-1941. In September 1941, Germany declared war on the Soviet Union, and the Nazis occupied Eastern Poland.

My formal schooling ended abruptly when I was twelve, in September 1941, with the German occupation of Grodno. I use the term schooling and not education, because I have continued my education on my own since that time. I spent four years in ghettoes and concentration camps, and shortly after the liberation, I tried to put my life together in post-war Europe—in Germany, Czechoslovakia, and England. I continued my self-education upon my arrival in this country in 1950.

The aforementioned facts have been expressed in order to clarify the reason for the absence of my formal schooling.

Up to the seventh grade in the Real-Gymnasium, I studied the prescribed curriculum. In addition to Polish, Russian, French, and Latin, I was also studying piano and drama. My parents instilled in me a deep sense of learning and respect for knowledge at an early age.

To me, education does not represent a piece of paper indicating the successful completion of a given course. I have studied throughout my adult life out of intellectual curiosity and a desire to broaden my knowledge in many diversified areas. I have, over the years, apart from continuous study of voice and music, attended evening classes in literature, languages, religion, and philosophy. I have formally studied voice, opera, and concert repertoire, and I made my professional debut in 1959 in New York City.

I have sung professionally in opera and on the concert stage. For the past twelve years, I have been on the faculty of the Settlement Music School. I have also been teaching voice and speech to students attending local universities, including the University of Pennsylvania, most of whom are involved with the Penn Singers.

My involvement with human rights led me to writing and speaking on the subject. I was approached by the Philadelphia School District Motivation Program to address numerous talks to area high schools. I have presented talks to professional groups and universities including Villanova and Cornell.

I am a member of the executive board of the Philadelphia Coordinating Council on the Holocaust,

Chairperson and Financial Secretary of Alumni and Friends of the Settlement Music School, and the press representative for the Philadelphia Singers.

The luxury of obtaining a formal education was not until now within my reach. For many years, I have harbored the dream of attending the University of Pennsylvania. Today, that dream may become a reality.

I would consider becoming a student at the University of Pennsylvania a great privilege and accept the challenge with a sense of deep commitment. I would look forward to the stimulus of a formal classroom, being able to exchange ideas and being part of the student body.

To bring a given goal to a successful conclusion, one needs discipline; courage in one's convictions; and a strong sense of commitment, coupled with diligent, focused, and serious work. These qualities have become inherent in my nature through circumstances and necessity. I have accomplished many goals I have set for myself through motivation and perseverance. Today, my passion for learning is stronger then ever.

I am aware that the University of Pennsylvania does not give credit for life's experiences. However, I am hoping that the Admissions Committee will take into consideration my particular background and accomplishments and make an exception. I would like to pursue studies in communication and criminology.

I am enclosing information about myself in addition to this letter that will give the committee a broader view of my background. I would be delighted should the committee find me a suitable candidate for admission to the University of Pennsylvania.

I received notification of my acceptance from the Dean and Director of Admissions who wrote, "I am pleased to inform you that you have been admitted to the College of General Studies beginning with the 1981 spring term." I was quite excited, to say the least. Me, the freshman at Penn! I enrolled in my first two courses almost immediately on my way toward my undergraduate degree. I chose Christian Origins and Russian Literature after 1860. Both courses were fascinating and very demanding.

I arrived at my first class in Russian Lit, and, carefully groomed, I entered the classroom at Williams Hall to a buzz of my young co-students. Naturally, I was very conscious of the fact that I was quite a bit older. The whole experience was so strange for me that I actually thought it was funny. I came home and wrote a sketch on my academic debut as a freshman without having ever attended a course of higher learning and without the benefit of having ever formally studied English.

First Impressions—Notes from the Undergrad
A sketch on my Academic Debut at the University of
Pennsylvania

January 13th 1981
　　Well, this is it, the culmination of a dream harbored for many years! I was going to attend my first class as freshman at the University of Pennsylvania, founded by Benjamin Franklin 240 years ago. To me, it seemed like 240 years away from my hometown of Grodno. Tonight was the night, and I thought of nothing else all day experiencing moments of real angst. The marvelous feeling of anticipation finally reached a full crescendo as I bravely walked toward Williams Hall.
　　I had a general idea where Williams Hall was, but I wasn't quite sure of the specific location. My mother used to tell me that God gave me a tongue. So, if you don't know, ask. I asked. A young man (Who else? They are all so young here.) was walking next to me. "Excuse me. Am I on the right track for Williams Hall?" (Neat way of phrasing a question if in doubt.)

126

"Yap" was the quick reply, "First building on the left. You can't miss it."

"Thanks," I responded with a shy smile. I was going to be just as brief, no need to waste precious words. Looking nonchalant, assuming the air of someone who is naturally accustomed attending academic institutions all my life, I entered Williams Hall looking for Room 102. I found it way down in the basement. So far, so good.

Wow, I thought, this is a long way from Grodno, and Grodno was never like this! If only my parents could see me now. From seventh grade to being a freshman at Penn, one of the most prestigious universities in the country, with nothing in between. What an academic jump. No fooling around for me, no siree! You want a formal education; start at the top. Who needs high school, right? Well, I hope you know what you are getting yourself into, I thought. Courage, girl, courage, you have lots of that, even if you did not finish grade school. Life prepared you for bravery. They don't bite here, do they? You have been in tight situations before. Yeah, I know, but this is different.

I found Room 102 – Russian Literature. No sweat. I walked in with confidence. After all, if I had stayed in Grodno, I would have read the thirteen assigned books of Russian literature in the original. Now I will do it in translation. Terrific! I am glad I know English.

As is my habit, I came to class a bit early. I found a few students in the classroom already shooting the breeze. They obviously knew each other and conducted an animated conversation. I looked around as more students entered the classroom. My God, they are so young! Practically babies. Well, you wanted to be a freshman. What did you expect? An old age home? I bet I know more than they do. I bet they haven't read as much Russian literature as I have. I gave myself a pep talk to keep my courage up. It is wonderful to converse with yourself. The questions and answers come simultaneously, so there is no time wasted. Time, such a precious commodity. And of course, everything was quite clear, except what the heck am I doing here and why am I experiencing a bit of angst?

The room kept filling with more students. They appeared perfectly relaxed, with not a care in the world. I began to observe the girls. My silent dialogue with myself continued. The first thing you must do is get yourself to the restroom and get rid of the lipstick. Nobody wears lipstick here. O.K. girl, self-adornment doesn't fit here, in this utopia of higher learning. Tomorrow when you come to class, you will wear your well-worn jeans, an old sweater and NO lipstick, that's for sure. Dress code, very important. Lesson number one. You want to be a freshman? Start looking like one. So what if I am old enough to be their mother?

I found out ahead of time what reading material was required for this course and came prepared with one of the thirteen books that were assigned for reading. A copy of Dostoyevsky's Notes from the Underground *was neatly tucked under my arm with a brand new notebook prominently displaying the words: Leges, Sine Moribus, Vanae—MY emblem! I suddenly became very possessive. University of Pennsylvania, founded by Benjamin Franklin 240 years ago, was now MY University. How about that! I haven't even started my first class, and it was already my university.*

Good quality, loyalty and pride. But first it would help to find out what those words really mean. It is befitting a freshman to be curious. I had Latin in fifth grade a hundred years ago and I forgot all of it. I proudly signed my name under those hallowed words.

The young co-student sitting next to me inquired whether I was getting my Ph.D. "Not yet," I answered in a matter-of-fact kind of way, "I am just starting my freshman year!"

Well, now I was ready to start absorbing all the wisdom from the wise professor, patiently waiting for his grand entrance. Not to appear too self-conscious, I began to scan the first chapter of Notes from the Underground, *underling sentences I considered pertinent to the inevitable term paper. But how will I know what is pertinent? Perhaps my wise professor will have different ideas about that. Well, perhaps I better wait for the wise professor to shed a light on my ignorance. My brand new yellow marker didn't do what it was supposed to do; smart as I am, I soon figured out that I was pressing the wrong end! Oh Nina, you are silly, and you have so much to learn. It would help to figure out how to use a marker properly for a start.*

Like a flash of lightning, an energetic young man dashed into the classroom. Why does he have to be so young too? He was the professor. He introduced himself briefly, and immediately started to pace the floor—a mile a minute. I was sure he was doing his daily walking exercises. He spoke rapidly, and in spite of the fact that I gave him my undivided attention, I could catch only one out of every third word. He was in a real hurry. The fact that he spoke with a strong Slavic accent didn't help much. Hey, wait a minute; look who's talking? Don't you speak with an accent? Well, maybe not an accent, but certainly with a foreign inflection.

The good professor pronounced the Russian authors and titles with a flair and perfection, but I knew he was not Russian. Well, I can certainly match him on pronunciation. That's a good start. He covered a great deal of material in a short time, outlined the basic expectations of the course, and informed the class that two major papers will be due on certain dates. Any questions? Are you kidding? I have about a dozen to start with, but of course I kept quiet not wanting to show my ignorance. I needed this course for my Humanities and Language credit, and I'd stick with it no matter how much work is involved. Good girl!

Notes from the Underground could not be classified as a "cheerful" work, to say the least. Having already tackled Tolstoy's The Death of Ivan Ilych and Solzhenitsyn's One Day in the Life of Ivan Denisovich, I found the Russians depressing to the point of utter despair. Oh, how they suffer! What a heavy dose of brilliant tragedy! And how they love to suffer! I suddenly remembered the comment my voice teacher, Lydia Chaliapin, daughter of the legendary Feodor, telling me in jest when I studied Tchaikovsky's Eugene Onegin (you see, I already read the masterpiece by Pushkin), "Darlink, I am only happy when I am miserable. That is the heart of the Russian soul." (Try that with a heavy Russian accent. It sounds better.)

Back home, I am now hastily jotting down my reflections to my academic debut. Armed with thirteen works of great literary merit by the great Russian writers, some of whom I hope will be more cheerful, I am ready to tackle Russian Lit course in earnest for the next thirteen weeks. Tomorrow, I will attend my first class in Religion—Christian Origins. The books of the New Testament are open and ready to be seriously dissected. That, and another thirteen books (I hope not) to peruse.

And tomorrow, I will know where Williams Hall is. I will look, well almost, like a freshman. Then maybe on the way to class someone will ask me where Williams Hall is, and with an air of total confidence, I'll reply "yap". No need to waste words, n'est pas? After this semester, I will need only thirty more credits to graduate. A staggering thought. But it could be fun, if I survive!

Penn was a challenge. I studied very diligently and received good grades. I read a great deal beyond the books and material connected with my research of the many diversified subjects. I spent countless hours in the library trying to make up for lost time in academia by thinking I could absorb all the extraordinary amount of material that takes others years to accumulate. To say that moments were trying would be an understatement. In my second course that first semester, Christian Origins, a fascinating subject that was of particular interest to me, the assigned material included writing four papers dealing with different aspects of Christianity in addition to writing an original research paper.

For my first paper, I chose to write a seven pager on the Jesus Traditions. I proudly submitted my paper to the professor expecting a pretty good grade. The following week I got my paper back with a grade of D minus! I looked at it with disbelief. My first reaction was, "You never wrote a paper. You don't know what the professor thinks should be included or excluded in that paper, and perhaps you should give up right now." I did not expect such a low grade. I thought it would be better than that.

I approached my professor and simply told him that this grade was not acceptable to me. He looked at me and replied, "I knew you would talk to me about this. You ask the most interesting questions; you pay the greatest attention; and you understand the material. You simply don't know how to structure an academic paper. You must learn how to substantiate and document your thoughts. You started very well and then got lost. Let me take you for coffee to the student lounge after class and I will try to explain how an academic paper should be structured."

I was very fortunate to have as one of my first professors a man of Dr. Kraft's ability as a teacher and as a man of great understanding. He recognized that I was a novice and helped me understand what I must do to write a comprehensive academic paper. Dr. Kraft made me re-write the paper a few times, and each time I felt more confident. I read the twenty-seven chapters of the New Testament with fervor, and then I studied the Synoptic Gospels to understand better the comparison between the writings of Mark, Matthew, and Luke.

For my original research paper, I decided to write on Paul (I was corrected by Dr. Kraft when I called him Saint Paul because we were dealing with first century Christianity and Paul was not referred to at that time as a saint.) "Paul's Perception of His Encounter with the Resurrected Jesus" took a lot of research, but I could only include primary sources. I could read but not include secondary sources, and I read many books about Paul by prominent writers to elucidate the complex personality of the man.

I was particularly interested in the role Paul played in the formation of the early Church. Paul's epistles, believed to be the earliest documented Christian writings, give us an insight to the question of who Paul was. So important was Paul's contribution to early Christianity that one third of the New Testament is devoted to him. I found the entire six-month course one of the most fascinating of that and other semesters. I also wanted to prove to myself that I could do better than a D minus! At the end of the semester, I received an A in the course. I also received an A in my Russian Literature class. Well, my cup was overflowing! I must credit Dr. Kraft for inspiring me to stick with my studies. I would have probably abandoned the idea of a formal university degree after one semester, feeling I could not make the grade, had I not received his encouragement.

It took me three years to complete half of my required courses because I was taking mostly evening classes and teaching during the day. I was drawn to subjects that dealt with religion in a historical setting and with the broad topic of criminology and sociology as seen in different societies and cultures. My interest in those subjects culminated in declaring Sociology as a major.

In one sociology course on deviance, I read Kai T. Erikson's *Wayward Puritans* that touches on the subject of deviance in society as it relates to the religious climate of early seventeenth century Massachusetts Bay. I was especially interested in the subject of the Antinomian Controversy and the trial of Mrs. Anne Hutchinson. After reading the transcripts of her trial, originally published in 1767 and reprinted by the Harvard University Press, as well as other related material pertaining to the Antinomian Controversy, I became totally engrossed in the subject. It became evident to me that events that had shaped America's early colonial days from 1630-1778 gave way to religious freedom, separation of church and state, and the subsequent birth of Civil Religion in America.

I have always been interested in the magnificent experiment of American democracy that will forever shine as a beacon and an example to the whole world, especially to self-appointed, hateful dictators. Reading and studying what was then considered deviant behavior gave me a greater understanding of how democracy and the brilliant vision of the Founding Fathers came about.

Out of the wilderness of John Winthrop and out of the turbulent days since the Antinomian Controversy, perhaps credit should be given to a brave and lone woman who helped spur the course of the American democratic principles and religious liberty as embodied in the Bill of Rights. Anne Hutchinson was fighting her own battles at that time, but how great would her victory have been had she known how much her participation contributed to the operative faith of the American people years later.

Anne Hutchinson was brutally tomahawked by a band of Indians on a late summer evening in 1643 in Rhode Island. Her legacy could be best described from the preamble of the Wisconsin Constitution: "We, grateful to the Almighty God for our freedom assert that the right of every man to worship according to the dictates of his own conscience shall never be infringed." If only the rest of the countries that practice abusive theocracy and terror by holding their people hostage would follow that preamble....

In 1983 I decided to take a Penn history course by attending the Venice Film Festival, the XL Mostra Internazionale del Cinema. It was a fascinating cinematic voyage to be able in a matter of eleven days to visit twenty-two countries and view thirty-five films. The Festival was at the service of filmmakers who conceived and participated in the actual execution of the production of their work. The auteur was encouraged to respond to the needs posed by the cinema of today—realism—and realistic it certainly was! Identity and familiarity of their indigenous cultures enabled the auteur to take the viewing audience on a socio-cultural travelogue.

Some of the films took us to the remotest places in the world or to the neighbors next door. The films exposed how society in general, and people in particular, cope with life and surroundings. We were exposed to ruthless upheavals, changing political climates, and state-imposed literary restrictions where freedom of expression is off limits. What I found particularly interesting was how the auteur attempted and often succeeded to define cinema's role in today's world in stark colors in the genre of cinema verite.

The topics covered a myriad of emotions: struggles for survival, people's dissatisfaction with their lives, people who run the risk of losing the little happiness they have by trying to get more, misplaced guilt, self doubt, passionate love, insanity, delusions, parental grief, frenzied daydreams and prostitution. It was all there. Adultery was seen not as a moral aberration, but as the invincible modus operandi of modern times. There was a stark absence of humor.

In the past, films essentially served the purpose of removing the viewer from reality. Today, the opposite is true. The days of the innocent, tender, light comedy and breezy romance have, for the most part, vanished from the screen. I was frankly looking for a bit of innocent fun amid all the realism. The overwhelming theme of the Festival in Venice dealt with the inanities of war and conflicts in societies on all levels. This topic came across vividly against the films that in the past depicted the lies that films used to portray.

Old-fashioned values and fidelity, the disappearing innocence; in this new wave of realism, it is the role of the film to act as the echo and mirror image of our civilization. The veil that obscured reality has been stripped away. The camera zoomed toward the center of things as they really are. Sex was almost a prerequisite, even if it was not relevant to the story line. Sexual scenes were not used in connection with tender love, but rather acting as a metaphor for the violent world outside.

Today, twenty years later, nothing has changed but is rather even more so. Nothing is sacred, and all is exposed. Resnais's La Vie Est un Roman" [Life is a Novel] was re-titled at the New York Film Festival as Life Is a Bed of Roses. Judging from the films of the Venice Film Festival '83, life is emphatically not. The auteur and director, often being the same person, tells us the way things really are and not the way we would like them to be.

Times produce social changes that are unmistakably incorporated into the making of films. We may wish for films to have happy endings and expect films to move from harsh realism to pleasant vignettes, but the world has lost its innocence and we are engulfed in lurid and cruel events. It seemed that during and after the Second World War, people's lives have become hopelessly twisted, and the new wave of realism starkly portrays true essentials.

Historical and political topics have always been favorite subjects encompassed in films. Governments are often depicted as sources of disorder that intrude into people's troubled lives. Arbitrary violence stems from the uncertainly and insecurity which is derived from political upheavals, and these upheavals are generally accompanied by meaningless brutality that takes a toll on the helpless citizens. Wars and revolution were treated as an important topic, and it became abundantly clear that the scars of the last two world wars have not healed. I could understand why the festival was chosen to be part of history studies. I learned a great deal in those eleven days, and I also explored in my free time the beauty, art, and rich history of Venice.

I was receiving mostly As and was anxious to move on academically toward a master's degree if that were possible. I didn't feel like spending another three years proving that I could academically achieve a full undergraduate degree, and I decided to speak to my counselor about that. She suggested that I should consider an associate degree, and I thought it was a good idea. I decided at that point to stop at that level, take a year off, and then apply to graduate school.

In September 1984, I received a letter from the Associate Dean and Director that read: "I am pleased to inform you that you were graduated from the Faculty of Arts and Sciences' College of General Studies on August 1984 and have been awarded the A.A. degree, Cum Laude. You should receive your diploma by mail in about eight weeks."

Eight weeks later I received my diploma from the University of Pennsylvania with a letter from the President of the University.

"I am very pleased to send you the diploma of the University of Pennsylvania, which admits you to the privileges and responsibilities represented by the earning of this degree. Congratulations on the successful completion of your course of study. As a student at the University, you have joined in a community dedicated both to the highest standards of learning and good citizenship. The Trustees and I, your teachers and advisors, hope that you will take much of value with you as you apply your talents to life in the society beyond Penn and your university years. The challenges will be many, but you will, I expect, meet them with strengths you did not know you possessed. You have my best wishes for personal happiness and for success in achieving the goals you set for yourself."

While I am sure the letter was sent to most graduating students, for me it held a very special meaning. Yes, President Hackney, I will face the many new challenges and hope to gather my inner strength and forge once again my courage and determination on my journey in life.

In 1986, the Association of Alumnae Board of Directors extended an invitation to me to speak during their annual meeting. I was really very touched when the description in the program read: Nina Kaleska: Teacher, performer, speaker, consultant, role model, scholar. Wow! Moi?

Since I was privately instructing students and business executives in public speech presentation and my natural ability was to communicate easily with people, I decided to pursue a master's in Communication. I investigated courses in that field at different universities that seemed to have exactly what I was interested in, and I decided to apply to Temple University in Philadelphia.

The process of applying to Temple was in itself a challenge. It is not customary going from an Associate degree directly for a master's, but then everything about my life and my academic experience did not follow the usual pattern. Why not try? Through a friend who was professor at Temple, I was introduced to the Chairman of the School of Speech and Communication. It was a most enlightening interview. He was impressed with my background and offered to intervene with the department on my behalf. I was asked to present seven letters of recommendation, and also conduct four interviews with different professors in the department.

The recommendation letters written on my behalf and the interviews resulted in my being accepted into the master's program in the department of Speech with emphasis on Rhetoric and Communication. One stipulation was that I had to maintain a B average, and I also had to take two undergraduate courses since I had no background in the subject on the undergraduate level. I couldn't wait to start. Before I graduated from Temple I wanted to write a postscript regarding my experience at Penn...

Many events have come to pass since the first scary days at Penn and my academic debut. Absorbing the scholarly wisdom in a frenzy to catch up all I have missed (academically) as a child, I was looking forward beyond undergraduate study. Time was precious, and my impatience mounting; I was ready to surge toward greater goals—graduate study. With the able help of my counselor, I decided to end my undergraduate stud-

ies with an associate degree and pursue a master's degree. Considering that I had never attended an English speaking school and was an elementary school "dropout" through no fault of my own, I unabashedly experienced a sense of accomplishment when, in my congratulatory letter from the President of the University, I was informed that I had graduated Cum Laude.

I remember fondly an encounter at Cohen and Kelly's, a restaurant on the Penn campus, one evening before a Sociology class when I was invited to join my professor who was dining with visiting foreign colleagues. The introduction went something like this, "This is Prof. X and Prof. Y and Prof. Z. And this, gentlemen, is one of my students, Nina Kaleska, scholar at large." Not bad. The words were music to my ears.

My old, electric typewriter on which I slaved away to prepare demanding research and term papers has been replaced by an obedient PC computer that I have almost mastered. I can actually verbalize in computer lingo.

My master's studies in Rhetoric and Communication at Temple University that I am shortly hoping to attain are very demanding. I could never have managed the tons of papers for the many diversified subjects in connection with human communication and behavioral sciences that are required in my program. Aristotle, Socrates, Plato, Cicero and Quintilian; the Art of Rhetoric, Human Communication Theory and other disciplines; forms and functions of persuasive speeches and research on rhetorical genre; many different approaches dealing with psychology and much more; all are neatly stacked away on my hard disc, ready to be retrieved with a mere switch of my finger. One wonders how the great thinkers of the past strolling and debating in the wide colonnades of ancient Forums were able to write their volumes of original thoughts without the benefit of our modern technology!

I had many frustrations and many questions regarding the grading system. Of course I knew that I understood the material of the texts, but some of my learned professors had different views on the matter. At one point, I was brave enough to write on the bottom page of one confusing exam on Psychology, for which I studied and practically memorized the 520 pages of information and whose test questions had little similarity to the material, "I know the answers. What is your question?"

Penn will always be a part of me. I feel devoted and proud to have been part of that great institution. I look at my unique learning experience from a different perspective than most of my younger colleagues do. I do not take for granted the opportunity to not only to study and learn but also to absorb, and I have had the opportunity to be exposed to the many diversified subjects of my choice. I worked hard to learn how to study and absorb the mountains of information.

Thank you, College of General Studies, for having faith in me and for providing the opportunity to embark on the road to achieve my academic goals. I am almost ready to finish my master's program and yes, I still have thirteen books in many of my courses, but I am no longer frightened. Since I find studying and learning exhilarating and challenging, I have caught the learning bug and will continue with additional academic studies, degrees or no degrees."

My extensive study pertaining to the subject of communications at Temple dealing with charismatic leadership, particularly political leadership, gave me an opportunity to explore the specific questions that have always intrigued me: How can one person achieve and eventually exert great power over a nation? Where does such power come from? How can one man change the course of history and destiny for a nation and subsequently engulf the world in his quest for total conquest?

The phenomenon of charismatic political leadership ultimately boils down to one word—persuasion. Without the ability to persuade, one could not inspire an entire populace and make a lasting impact on a society for better or for worse. What is it about some individuals that can inspire, spellbind, and seduce multitudes? What charismatic properties make up the personalities of those who are successful in their quest for domination? What ultimately produces a charismatic phenomenon?

Since these questions were always puzzling me and I was frankly fascinated with the subject, I devoted a great deal of time researching the material. Some of the answers I found in my studies on charisma, persuasion, philosophy, and rhetoric.

Max Weber, the eminent German sociologist, named *Fuehredemokratie*, a type of devotion and trust that a populace embraces in a leader who is seen as having the ability to rescue the nation from distress in time of exigency. The most spectacular leader promises the greatest results and employs the most effective propaganda by repeatedly pointing to despair that only he can transform into utopian state.

The leader must continue to prove his ability to create and promote a single event within a social, political, or religious movement; he must infuse it with new and different ideals that must inspire his followers or transform his charismatic vision into a totally new order. Domination and authoritarian power is viewed as axiomatic. He seizes a given task and demands obedience from his followers. His didactic messages and authority become distinctly personal. Hitler was a master in audience manipulation by constantly using agitating, bombastic speeches full of repetitive clichés infused with stale phrases that served to produce an uncritical response.

Even after 2500 years, I found the speeches of the Roman orator and statesman Cicero so fitting to our own times: "Nothing in oratory is more important than to win for the orator the favor of his listeners and to have the latter so affected as to be swayed by something resembling a mental impulse or emotion, rather than by judgment or deliberation. For men decide far more problems by hate or love or lust or rage or sorrow or joy or hope or fear or illusion or some other inward emotion than by reality or authority or any legal standard." Nothing has changed in over 2000 years when it comes to persuasion in the political arena…

The successful orator taps into a reservoir of folklore, myths, and heroes, and he projects himself in these figures. A scapegoat is always a safe way to infuse an audience to hysteria: blame someone else, particularly people against whom emotions can be easily aroused, for one's woes. In Hitler's reigns, the Jew was the convenient and omnipotent scapegoat. He twisted this emotion to extremes and used anti-Semitism as a backbone to build his Nazi empire.

Hitler was probably the greatest manipulator in audience response. He understood the power of persuasion and passion. Parts of his speeches were so sufficiently vague and ambiguous; they could be interpreted that to disregard his authority and his warnings was to invite calamity. F.G. Bailey remarks in his *Tactical Uses of Passion* that "there can be no purposeful activity without emotion or without passion. Reason has no power to move; without passion one remains inert, unmoved and unable to move others." Hitler was able to strike a chord through his verbal style in combination with his exaggerated body movements that together were able to whip up his followers to hysterical, enthusiastic outbursts. It was drama at its highest level!

But what would history be like if every amateur, dilettante historian wrote versions according to subjective interpretations? History records what happened in a society at a given time so that future generations can learn. It should involve painstaking research and well-founded evidence. Without correct reporting, the legacy left behind by historians would become biased misrepresentations of the truth.

In 1986, the French government ordered a full-scale investigation into the granting of a doctoral degree by Nantes University to a candidate whose thesis claimed that the gas chambers were a figment of "Jewish imagination" and the

Holocaust in fact did not occur. The writer decided that the gas chambers were used for sanitary purposes to prevent the spread of epidemics. The Germans, the author claimed, "are a very clean people." The author was Henri Rogues, a retired sixty-five-year old agricultural engineer and amateur historian.

The Ph.D. thesis was rejected after it was brought to the attention of sixty Nantes University faculty members who protested its acceptance. While people have a right to publish their views, the granting of degrees, doctoral or any other, based on distortions of documented facts should provoke indignation and genuine concern in academia. Did Rogues ever see the documentary film *Night and Fog* by his countryman, Alain Resnais? That should have forever dispelled the doubt that gas was used for sanitary purposes!

Similar literature that has continued to repeat the canard has appeared in a number of European countries and in America. In 1977, Arthur Butz, professor of electrical engineering at Northwestern University, published a book flatly denying the Holocaust. All one can say is that it is history that never happened written by people who were never there!

These writers who revise history to promote a subjective and warped ideological course are turning the Holocaust into deliberate distortions and virulent rhetoric. They are obsessed with twisting the truth, the purpose of which is to perpetrate fallacies and employ a standard propaganda tactics so successfully used by the Nazis and their hero, Hitler. Yell loud and often, use bombastic rhetoric, spread the lies, and people will start believing and be persuaded to their cause.

My May 1988 graduation ceremony from Temple touched me more than I thought it would. I wrote a letter to Dr. Towne, my Philosophy professor who was the Chairman of the department, when I originally applied and who was very supportive in my admission process. He and his wife invited me for a long weekend to their summer home in Maine but I could not join them. I wrote the following:

My graduation
Temple University – 1988

May 19 came and went. The day was filled with a strange feeling of nostalgia and bittersweet feelings in spite of the fact that I did not place that much emphasis on the whole graduation affair. I did not join the circus at the Spectrum [a former Philadelphia indoor stadium] where the main ceremonies were being held, but I did attend the graduation in the afternoon for the College of Arts and Sciences. When my name was called and the Dean handed me my diploma, my eyes did tear up a bit. I wished that my parents could have seen me.

During my last years of studies, I found that some of the professors, the younger breed of professors, despite excellent academic credentials, do not have the vision that education on a higher level entails more than writing good papers. Originality of thought is often not appreciated. They seem to stick to a prescribed formula and rarely deviate beyond the material at hand.

One of my Penn professors came to the Temple graduation commencement and I was really touched by that. During the reception, someone must have mentioned something about me to the Dean, and the next day, I received a phone call from the Temple Times *Public Relations department. With great apologies that "We are sorry that we didn't know about you," (why would they?) a young reporter asked for an interview.*

If something is published, I will send you a copy. Your kind invitation to join you at your Golden Pond *sounds divine and, depending on my schedule, I just might take you up on your offer. Studying with you and getting to know you was such a special pleasure. I want you to know that I have bought myself a special graduation present: the works of Aristotle and Plato.*

A producer friend who urged me to audition for the part of the Abbess in the Broadway revival of The Sound of Music *phoned last week to say that the part*

144

was given to a well-known international actress. As he put it, she is twice as big in size as I am and her voice is a true contralto, which of course I am not. She has already done the part on Broadway. He was very complementary about the audition but I told him if I were the casting director, I would not have cast me in that role. I really had no illusions about becoming involved in the theatre at this stage of my life. It was nevertheless a challenge and a compliment to be asked to audition for such a major production on Broadway, but I was frankly relieved.

I shall miss you at my "graduation party" but am glad that we had a chance to get together before you left. I hope your summer is filled with balmy days.

Chapter 11

Before Cardinals and Colleges

In 1973, many years before I embarked on my academic career,
I was invited to participate at a Holocaust symposium that featured
prominent scholars and theologians of different religious persua-
sions. The invitation came from Dr. Katsh, the President of
Dropsie University, a prestigious Philadelphia institute that pro-
motes scholarship and research among top academics nationwide.
Dropsie co-sponsored this symposium with Villanova University,
a Catholic University in Villanova, Pennsylvania.

Dr. Katsh approached me after a dinner party at a mutual
friend's home and said, "I have read your article that was published in London (included in the Abyss chapter) and found it
extremely touching. It is an important human document. You
have something very important to share with the rest of us. Our
colloquium is the first of its kind in Philadelphia. I want you to
write a purely subjective paper directed to sources of human
resistance: specifically, how you got to Auschwitz, what happened to you, and how you were able to remain sane during
those years." It was quite a request, to say the least.

It took me a while to digest what he asked. He smiled at me
and said, "Well, what about it?"

"That's quite a tall order," I answered. "All you want me to
do is bare my life publicly and re-live a painful period of my life

146

I am trying to forget. You must understand that the article I wrote in London was written shortly after the war. In a sense, it was a letter to myself."

"Yes", he answered, "You now have a responsibility as an eyewitness to relate subjectively an important and tragic part of our living history. I would really like you to participate. It will be an important joint venture and a dialogue between Christians and Jewish scholars. Your contribution will be very important." Dr. Katsh encouraged me by pointing out that I was sharing thoughts on a historic and psychological perspective as only an eyewitness can.

I participated in that scholarly symposium and shared the platform with cardinals, bishops, and learned professors. I was the only one without a Ph.D. It was also the only time I have given a purely subjective paper about my experiences. My paper was titled "Sources of Human Resistance"

After relating the specifics of my life in the Grodno ghetto, my two years at Auschwitz, and then subsequent incarceration at Ravensbruck and Restow, I concluded with the following thoughts:

> *Psalm 55 from the Book of Psalms expressed how I felt in those days: "Let Death seize upon them and let them go down quickly into hell for wickedness is in their dwelling." How often I cursed my captors with those words. And in many private conversations with God, I would ask how He could witness such suffering and let innocent people die in great agony. Why? Why?*
>
> *Again, from Psalm 55: "Fearfulness and trembling are come upon me and horror hath overwhelmed me. As for me, I will call upon God and the Lord shall save me." The Lord did save me, but what about the millions of innocent victims whose only crime was to be born a Jew? How could I justify my own survival? I felt an inner rebellion for a long time. I could not go into a synagogue because the memories of our own*

beautiful synagogue in Grodno, its destruction and the purpose for which the Nazis used it, were too vivid in my mind. It was too painful for me to hear the rabbi pray and the cantor chant. I was the youngest and weakest of an extended family. Why me? I still cannot answer that question. I would quietly walk into a synagogue or a church when no one was there, sit alone in the back, and talk to God. I still do. Through the Holocaust years, first with my sister and then alone, I would pray against hope that somehow, someday, maybe I would be reunited with my parents.

Many years later when I visited Yad Vashem, the memorial to the six million Jews in Jerusalem, my first reaction shocked me. When I entered that incredible shrine and saw the coffin with the single reef on it and I saw the names of each concentration camp carved on stone and illuminated by an eternal light, my eyes rested on Auschwitz.

Once again, my hell became alive. I broke down and couldn't face it. For years I had submerged my feelings, and confronted by the past so suddenly, I fell apart. In freedom, I could not control my emotions.

When I returned to Yad Vashem for a second time a few years later, I told my husband that I needed to visit the memorial alone. I remembered everything and stood for a long time looking at the coffin. It was for me a reunion with my parents and sister. I needed to be alone with my memories. Now I am anxious for my children to visit Yad Vashem. I know they cannot feel what I have felt, but I want them to know and become aware of the tragic past. We must not forget.

In trying to determine how I survived the Holocaust and what kept me sane, I must first say that my being here is a miracle. By all odds, I should not have survived. But who am I to argue with fate? My own will to survive must have been very strong, aided by my deliberate unawareness of the shocking tragedy that has been a part of my life.

Only years later when I was able to analyze what had actually happened did I realize the improbability of my own survival. Reality was unbearable at the time. I can think and talk about my past today because I remember the past, but live in the present and think about the future. The resilience required to adjust to a normal, functioning life after the shocking horror of the recent past takes a strong will and intensely positive thinking.

I used to find a little ray of hope each morning and tell myself that I would make it through the day. In my imagination, I would play in our beautiful park where I spent many hours as a child. Imagination is a powerful tool for survival. I have been witness to man's greatest inhumanity to man. Now we must talk about it and inform people so that it is not forgotten. Forgetting is dangerous. This horrible crime against humanity must never happen again. It is our responsibility to let everybody know. The suffering and death of millions of people must not go in vain. We must learn a lesson, no matter how painful it may be to hear about it."

Ever since the publication of my Dropsie talk, the subject of the "survivor" (I hate the word!) had stimulated uncommon interest. As a result, I was repeatedly invited to address area high schools, civic organizations, and churches. My reluctance to take on the role of an eyewitness narrator overshadowed my feelings of apprehension. I accepted the responsibility with a heavy heart.

For the next few years, I accepted invitations in an attempt to make a contribution in any small way, to enlighten those who knew little about that time in history. Judging by the reaction of the listeners—whether high school or college students, church and synagogue audiences, or university professors—my talks were received with great interest and appreciation. I felt that it was important for all of us to understand the struggle of subjective experiences in an attempt to resist horror and tyranny at a time when the world became mute.

I put my feelings aside and agreed to speak. Agreeing to speak is one thing, doing research and writing about it took a toll. It became a difficult task. It was painful to spend many weeks deliberately recalling personal events during the dark ages of my life. Talking about my private hell was not going to educate people, and I was not willing to share many painful recollections publicly. The Dropsie talk was the exception to the rule. In subsequent talks I concentrated on the political, psychological, and sociological developments by pointing out how that gigantic catastrophe evolved and came about. The Holocaust did not come out of a void.

In 1975, I received an invitation from the Ministry of Villanova University to be the main speaker during the Sunday six o'clock Eucharistic Mass in the beautiful and gigantic St. Thomas Church. Standing under a cross, surrounded by seven white robed priests, Father Driscoll, the President of the University, introduced me in a most eloquent manner. I faced a congregation of over 900 people!

A few years later I received an invitation from Cornell University as a weekend "scholar in residence". I was to address a Sunday morning Mass at Sage Chapel, the oldest interdenominational chapel in American academia; lead a discussion with students at lunch; and share an evening with the faculty. I experienced a sense of angst since at that time I officially had only a seventh grade level schooling. I spent weeks preparing for the challenge. The morning talk was broadcast over the Syracuse-Ithaca area the following Sunday. The many letters and positive comments from the students and faculty made the experience very gratifying.

I arrived home from Ithaca exhausted and pensive. The phone rang as I entered my house. "Hi Mom, how did it go?" My younger son was checking up on his mom.

"Very illuminating, interesting and exhausting," I answered. "I really can't do this thing too often; it is too draining."

"I know," he said. "You are making an important contribution, and you do it so well." We chatted for a while and I told him the events of the weekend, the reaction of the students and faculty, and my thoughts about the experience.

"It's a beautiful campus; I wish you could take your graduate studies there."

"Go get yourself a cup of tea, put on a Mozart symphony, and relax," he replied. I took my son's suggestion. Mozart's Symphony No. 40 was very soothing. The music permeated the house, and I was beginning to feel relaxed. I went upstairs to my study with teacup in hand.

My life has been shaped by negative and very difficult experiences, but I have chosen not to make them its focal point. How does one go beyond survival and turn difficult and potentially devastating experiences into opportunities for personal growth and, to some extent, triumph? I was part of that generation that saw the past century both glorious and damned… a century that has seen humanity through unprecedented horrors, a century that has seen new and important scientific discoveries and amazing exploration of the outer limits. This century has witnessed two world wars and many regional catastrophes that have carried devastation to the far corners of every continent of the planet.

The chronicles of human wreckage appear to be well documented, but we have not learned sufficiently from history. Hitler envisioned his Reich to last a thousand years. It lasted twelve years and was soundly defeated, but the spores still survive and seem to multiply, albeit in mutation, adopted by countries that practice cruel theocratic fundamentalism for their own gain, always, of course, in the name of God and religion.

The essence of Hitlerism—ethnic hatred, extreme national-ism, and state-organized and condoned murder—is sadly still alive. Fanatically anti-democratic movements arise and flourish, killing millions of innocent people, often in their own countries. These self-imposed and self-appointed dictators who gain polit-ical power emulate Hitler, but Hitler's impact went beyond his willingness to kill without mercy or reason. He did something civilization had not seen before. With his racial laws, he set out to create an Aryan Valhalla for the pure Aryan race, whatever that means. The Nazis killed people not for what they did, but for who they were, for just being born! Hitler and his henchmen killed over a million Jewish children just for existing.

After the war, the world learned the enormity of the crimes perpetrated by the Nazis in the name of the German people. We should be asking the question, what have we learned from those catastrophic events? Would genocide be so rampant and readily embraced by the current crop of dictators if nations understood the horrors of the past? There has been a lot of dialogue, but not enough action and even less understanding.

Since I had the opportunity to address many colleges, uni-versities, churches and civic groups during the 70s and 80s, I have always felt very strongly that there was a genuine interest related to the subject of the Holocaust and World War II in general. When I would accept an invitation to speak, I injected less about myself and focused more on what hatred and igno-rance produced. What happens when the handwriting is on the wall but people do not get the message until it is too late? In reality, what happens in one country sooner or later does even-tually affect everyone.

In November of 1988, the Neumann Center of Villanova University sponsored the Catholic Neumann Province Conference. The theme that year was "Reconciliation in Today's World." I was invited to spend one afternoon during a three-day retreat with Catholic students who came from area universities and colleges. At first, I felt reluctant since I had not engaged in "talks" for some time, and I became even more reluctant when I was asked specifically to address the topic of "Finding Peace Within Yourself."

Six months before, in May that year, I had received my master's in Rhetoric and Communication from Temple University and, having recently graduated and still feeling like a student myself, I felt that I could relate to a group of students and share my thoughts about my life and academia. But of course, broaching a subject like "Finding Peace within Yourself" was a bit touchy.

Finding peace within oneself? Well, I set my goals and finished my studies, but I was not sure how much I was at peace with myself. I was faced with a new challenge again—armed, this time, with new academic credentials, I was trying to find the right job from scratch, at my age. Of course I felt uncertain and not particularly at peace. But I had been there before, faced many challenges and managed to step over hurdles and achieve satisfaction.

I thought about what I could impart to the students and then I decided to accept their invitation, realizing that I had something to share with them. In preparation for the conference, I searched into my self in the hope that I could understand my own strength and relate to others what emotional component made my unlikely survival possible. In so doing, I wanted to discover from where inner strength derives in order to cope with adversity. Finding inner peace is an ongoing process.

I arrived at the retreat and spent an entire afternoon sharing my own and their thoughts with them. The session was quite informal. People were sitting on chairs or sofas and tables, and many sat on the floor scattered around the room. The atmosphere was one of friendship. I was introduced, and I was somewhat surprised that a few had remembered my talk at St. Thomas' Church on the campus of Villanova University when the ministry invited me to speak during a Sunday Eucharistic Mass. The group seemed predisposed to hear what I had to share with them. There were about sixty students, ranging from freshmen to Ph.D. candidates. They came from all walks of life and different backgrounds. They all had one strong point in common: they were all Catholics from different regional universities and colleges attending their special three day retreat. These are some of the reflections I shared with them.

Reconciliation in Today's World—Finding Peace, within Yourself

When I was invited to share with you part of this weekend, it gave me the opportunity to reflect on some aspects of my life and to probe for a deeper meaning in search of the ubiquitous notion of finding inner peace, the topic you requested me to talk about. The spirit of fostering reconciliation and understanding led me into my own introspective self-analysis. Studies in behavioral psychology have shown that the things we love are very brittle, while the things we hate remain very strong. Assumptions about ourselves and of others exert a profound influence on the beliefs and expectations that make up our world and inner needs. I will attempt to share with you some of the experiences that made me function in absence of moral and spiritual support under very difficult and unusual circumstances.

Ultimately, how can one translate the intensification of inner life from a refuge of emptiness, desolation, and spiritual poverty to find inner peace? How does one find a meaning for suffering and press on with life? In my own experience, the path leading to inner peace was paved by endurance of great suffering and also in accepting the reality that I was caught up in a nightmare. I came to terms that my life was very dramatic, and I do not by any means compare my tribulations of a place like Auschwitz with those I have to face in daily life today.

For me, experiencing dissatisfaction and anger became a prelude to courage. Without knowing it, I have practiced the Freudian defense mechanism of sublimation where, according to Freud, one takes the impulse from the id and changes it to a more positive activity, the healthy ego. Feelings of disappointment and pain, which are unavoidable in life, are often a first step that leads to overcoming psychological discomforts, and self-analysis starts with facing up to the truth.

I have often questioned God's plan for my unlikely survival against insurmountable odds. I argued with Him. It took me years before I could go to a synagogue because I felt like a stranger in my own house. I was fighting a personal battle. The pain of separation and death of my parents and sister, the years of endurance of indignities and humiliation by beasts dressed in men's clothing left me with a deep mark of suffering.

With time, I have reconciled my pain. What I am still searching for are the broader philosophical questions connected with the meaning of suffering and the never-ending question: why? In spite of having been a witness to a great catastrophe, I am grateful that life did not make me bitter, pessimistic, arrogant, or anti-religious. The human capacity to transcend difficult predicaments can be achieved by reconciling, accepting, and coping with fate.

The Holocaust was an event of such enormous magnitude that an ordinary person who did not experience it is incapable of its shocking reality. I can only attempt to raise this experience to a transcendental plane to describe that which is almost not possible to comprehend in order to tolerate the memories.

It is essential to understand that the implications of the Holocaust in its relation to our lives today—the mark carved on civilized man as a result of that catastrophe—is more relevant than ever. Were the Holocaust to remain the province of only those who were direct witnesses, it would not become a critical warning for the rest of the world. It was not just an event of the past, but it created forever a challenge to humanity's conscience. It is a challenge to faith. Judaism and Christianity are both religions of redemption: for the Jews, the Exodus and Sinai; for the Christians, the death and resurrection of Jesus.

When I speak of the Holocaust, it is not possible to say that I have reconciled with that tragedy, and I find it difficult to view the event objectively. I believe that the Holocaust should not be viewed in terms of guilt or revenge; it should be approached and studied as means to a greater understanding of twentieth century history; what happens when a civilized society demonstrates its collective indifference and when the rest of the world ignores obvious warning signs.

Lessons of the Holocaust should be taught as an important part of history, philosophy, psychology, and religious thought. The subject requires greater expansion for sociological research and recognition that in Nazi Germany not only God, but also the established Christian religion and any notion of justice were all to be killed. Nazism became the new religious order, and the swastika the new cross.

In Auschwitz, I ceased to be a human being; I became a number. There had been no precedent in modern history where a sentence of death was imposed on anyone guilty of having been born.

We carried our death certificates on our left forearm, from which only the date was missing. That was our reality.

At birth, I became a person, then a number, and then a person again. After my liberation, I had to learn how to cope with the world as a free human being. I didn't understand why I was singled out to survive my entire family, and I viewed my existence as a miracle that left me with a sense of responsibility as an eyewitness to share my experiences and enlighten those who know little about that time in history. Knowledge not shared is lost forever. As dramatized by Auschwitz, the tragedy has shown that it was not about what some people were capable of doing to the Jew. Rather, it was about what some people were capable of doing to other people in absence of social responsibility and total abandonment of moral or ethical conduct. Laws were created solely to suit the political climate.

Conventional wisdom teaches that in the metaphysical realm, the world relies on orderliness and rationality. Otherwise, there is a sense of absurdity in human existence. What happens when part of the species goes berserk and comes up with evil rulers? The metaphysical realm is also composed of opposites: dark and light, as well as right and wrong.

The dynamic forces of good and evil constantly vie for the soul of man. Throughout the ages, writers and poets have been fascinated with this ubiquitous theme. In literature, particularly notable is Goethe's immortal Faust and the resulting consequences of trading one's soul with the devil for a promise of temporary earthly pleasures. The other is Shakespeare's Othello dealing with the corrupt character of Iago who identifies himself with Satan. In his monologue, the Credo, Iago declares: "Foul is the seed I come from, filthy and rotten is all that's in me... I must go my evil path with him...I am an obedient tool of my demon's will... my vile intent must never cease nor weaken 'ill it has reached its goal."

We often promise according to our hopes and perform according to our fears. Humans have both the highest potential for goodness, and we also posses the highest potential for evil, as has been dramatically demonstrated by Hitler. Evil is not the creation of God but the invention and greed executed by people.

In this century and in my own experience, literally millions of innocents were the victims of the evil called Nazism. That evil spirit became the Credo of the Nazi party that flourished in the midst of one of the most highly developed and civilized societies. Just like Othello, who did not recognize Iago's motives until it was too late, so too the Western world did not question Nazi philosophy until its doom was sealed.

Today's events are the results of yesterday's history. Nazi philosophy did not come out of a void. Religiously rooted anti-Semitism provided an effective vehicle for transmitting biased information directed at the Jews, not by Christianity but by Christians who chose to use the Cross as a symbol of persecution.

In 1973, I was invited by Dropsie University to participate in a Scholars' Colloquium on the Holocaust, and I was asked to present a purely subjective paper of my experiences in the Nazi camps, particularly of my two years in Auschwitz. I was at first very reluctant to accept the invitation, for it meant recollecting very difficult and painful years of my youth. It would force me to retrieve memories that had lain dormant for many years. I locked myself in my study for three weeks and kept writing. For a while I led two lives; I was back in the camps, and I also functioned as a mother, wife, and career woman.

When I finished my paper, it occurred to me that the everyday annoyances I faced were almost insignificant in comparison. I kept rationalizing that if I could have gone through that experience, I could accept anything! But that is not true. Everything is relative. I don't believe in prisoner mentality. If one cannot adjust to different life situations, one cannot function productively, and ultimately, one can never find inner peace.

Among the distinguished Catholic scholars that day at the Dropsie Symposium were Cardinal Krol, Father Papin, and Father John Driscoll, who shortly after was appointed President of Villanova University. Father Driscoll's words still echo in my mind when he said, *"One of the things that I have sensed in these proceedings is the over-riding presence among us of an unalterably firm belief in the One God. We believe in the same God... The unity we find in our Judeo-Christian tradition highlights the truth that we not only share a common origin, but even more comforting, we acknowledge the purpose of human existence of this day and all that it commemorates."*

For me, Father Driscoll's concluding words that day led to a feeling of inner reconciliation and a degree of inner peace. It was for me a magnificent revelation. He continued, *"The sense of our openness, the genuine willingness to open our lives so that others may enter have called forth one of the most pitiable and most glorious of human gestures, that of reaching out to another human being."* His talk evoked echoes of the past and visions of a better future, of finding inner peace through reconciliation and mutual understanding and through a willingness to acknowledge that Christians and Jews have entered into a new and unique relationship.

The process of reconciliation is a process of conversion within your own self and through inner searching. I don't believe life owes you anything unless you are willing to become involved, contribute, and try to make a difference. When I was attempting to cope with my survival, I felt at times a sense of guilt for having been the only one of my family to survive. Coping with guilt belongs in the realm of reconciliation. But how does one argue with fate? Personal reconciliation breaks down the barriers of hostility. To forgive those who have wronged you is noble but not always easy, especially when the scars of injustice can never completely heal.

As a result of my participation at the Dropsie symposium and publication of my talk, I was invited to address many Christian audiences. One such occasion was in 1975 when the Ministry of Villanova University gave me the unique honor of addressing a six o'clock Sunday Mass. The subject of my "sermon" was "Subjective Reflections of the Post-Holocaust Years."

In preparation for such an auspicious event, I found a supplication in an old book of prayers: "O Lord of the Universe, it is revealed before Thy throne of glory that I am obliged to speak in public." But it wasn't just any public. It was a Catholic Church filled with over 900 Catholic congregants, and I, a Jew, a survivor of the Holocaust, was going to stand on the pulpit under a Cross, that all-embracing symbol of love and compassion which became instead for the Jews of Europe a disturbing and frightening sight. The cross on which Jesus died became for Jews over many centuries a sign of fear and persecution, of ghettos and discrimination, of raids and pogroms. And all those ultimately led to the greatest recorded human tragedy in the civilized world. The cross no longer holds terror for me. In religion, one finally comes to recognize what binds people together and reconciles the strong common bond between Christians and Jews in an ecumenical spirit.

My participation in this assembly is in itself very significant. It expresses the deeper meaning of promoting a genuine interfaith dialogue in the spirit of reconciliation. Reconciliation, whether personal or religious, ultimately leads to greater inner peace through understanding of oneself and others. It would be presumptuous of me to suggest that I can give you an easy formula for finding inner peace, but perhaps sharing some segments of my life will help illuminate that in coping with difficulties with a positive attitude, one can overcome many hurdles and find a new perspective toward life.

The spirit of reconciliation and the relationship of the Church to non-Christian religions came about as a result of the Declaration *Nostra Aetate* issued by the Second Vatican Council in October 1965. It marks an important watershed and milestone in the history of Jewish-Christian relations. After almost 2000 years often marked by mutual ignorance and frequent confrontations, the declaration provided a unique opportunity to reconcile and heal wounded feelings. It brings forth a deeper understanding and concerns of mutual awareness and open dialogues based on trust and respect.

Last Wednesday, Cardinal John O'Connor of New York asked all 410 churches in his Archdiocese to ring their bells and for parishioners to light candles to remember the fiftieth anniversary of *Kristallnacht*, the Night of Broken Glass in 1938 when Nazi destruction of Jewish shops and synagogues throughout Germany was met with stone silence from ordinary Germans and the nations of the outside world, an event that signaled a green light for Hitler's goal of total elimination of the Jewish people. That commemoration was also observed in major cities in this country and more amazingly, throughout Germany and other nations of Europe. For me personally, the event was striking in its significance. It was not only a gesture of reconciliation but a living reality.

In search of inner peace, it is first necessary to acknowledge that life is composed of conflicts and resolutions. Reconciliation is a process of resolutions whether these conflicts are personal, religious, or social. Experiencing stress and coping with difficulties is a normal daily activity. Only someone who walks through life as a zombie, or one who deliberately excludes and avoids any challenges feels no pain.

There is a saying that there are those who make things happen, those who watch things happen, and those who never knew what happened. To reconcile is also to forgive, but there is a difference between forgiveness and reconciliation. Forgiveness implies a kind of moral embrace. Reconciliation is a transaction, in coming to terms with one's own feelings and understanding and the role we play in this world.

Shortly after the war when I was faced with the reality that I survived the Holocaust, my impatience in wanting to change the world right away was that of a typical young girl. Somehow, and unexplainably, the frightening existence of my youth in Nazi camps did not dampen by enthusiasm for life and belief in people. I could have stayed angry, but I realized even then that in order to function, I needed to reconcile my fate and attempt to understand where I was in life.

Living with hate is very destructive. I was guided by my own conscience and had to make my own choices. And because to err is human, I often made the wrong choices. But with maturity one also acquires patience and the realization that changes take time; learning to accept trials and coping with difficulties are part of life. I believe that my willingness to persevere when realities looked very bleak made the difference in my life. I did not have the luxury of indulging in self-pity.

In June 1945, I embarked in Prague, Czechoslovakia, after a three-day bus ride from a refuge camp somewhere in Germany. I found myself standing alone and feeling very isolated. What was so painfully striking was the reality that my fellow travelers were met by members of their families and friends. I stood aside, alone and frightened, wondering what purpose God had for me first to witness the destruction of my people and then to test my strength and endurance to re-enter the world again. What happened subsequently is too long to go into details at this time, but through strange circumstances, I spent the next three months being cared for by nuns in a convent.

I learned about the war after the war, and only much later, when I began to read historical accounts, did I grasp the enormity of the crime perpetrated on the Jewish population of Europe. I read with horror the tons of authenticated evidence that deluged in truckloads at the International Military Tribunal in Nuremberg in 1946. The trials exposed horrendous war crimes and opened to history a detailed inside account of the corruption of absolute power. The trials forever shook the complacency of a Western culture that had overestimated the depth of its civilized qualities and endless possibilities of evil.

When I came to understand my own experience, I also realized that I carried a special responsibility as a witness. Deep reflection of those dreaded years left me with a sense of commitment to contribute even in a small way because knowledge not shared is lost forever. Today, revisionists are trying to re-write history. This process can be described as a history that never happened written by people who were never there.

Two thousand years ago, Aristotle wrote that to attain knowledge about the soul is the most difficult task in the world. To live, to suffer and to find meaning in the suffering is an art that we have not yet defined. From my own experience, I carry a sense of wonderment of the resources of the human spirit to have emerged from a dark abyss in the face of tremendous adversity and still have found hope in humanity. Out of bigotry that I have experienced so deeply, I have attempted to understand a burning vision of human potential for good to match the evil.

Finding peace within oneself is ultimately a relative process. Inner peace is an umbrella term that signifies many emotions. It is transient, depending on given circumstances. It helps to look at people with really serious problems and to compare their circumstances with ours to realize that we often exaggerate our own self-importance. Perhaps you have heard the expression, "I saw a man without shoes, and then I saw a man without feet."

We all cope with stress in our own manner. Reflecting, meditating and gathering spiritual resources help us function more productively. I have found that quiet and earnest meditation leads me to a state of inner tranquility. I try to forgive when I was wronged because holding grudges makes me uncomfortable. To forgive is noble but not always easy to do. It takes strength to reason and forgive.

Learning how to discriminate between right and wrong is rational thinking. Much of life for most of us is spent dealing with the gaps between what we want and what we get. I don't think you can find inner peace through someone else; you must first find it within yourself and only then can you share that feeling. You can come to terms with life if you face reality and ultimately take responsibility for your own actions. Don't expect to have someone else solve your problems for you.

In moments of great stress, I usually become very calm. When I was actively singing, I was always puzzled that a day or two before a performance I became sleepy and lethargic. I thought I would never be able to function in this state. But something amazing always happened.

When I came on the stage and faced the audience, my adrenalin flowed. I felt completely in control and performed well. It was as though my body was storing all the energy and nervous tension I needed to perform. I believe that we have a built-in defense mechanism that protects us in daily life that helps us cope with difficulties. I call that my reservoir of inner strength. I have come to rely on it.

Eight years ago when I decided to pursue an academic degree, I experienced the usual stress that goes with the endless assignments, submitting papers on time, and preparing for final exams. A paper that I was sure deserved an A was marked only a B plus. I learned to take it in stride and recognize that you cannot always please someone else, particularly professors. I made a serious commitment to learn and do well academically. But even more importantly, I derived great satisfaction from just acquiring a great deal of knowledge, and I stood up to the challenge, particularly since I entered my undergraduate studies with the equivalent of a seventh grade schooling and have never formally studied English.

There were occasions when I had legitimate reasons to argue with the professor and get a higher mark. Was it ultimately that important? I rationalized that professors often want you to absorb in a matter of four months the assigned material that took them a lifetime to accumulate. I was so frustrated at one point during a trying psychology test dealing with purely hypothetical questions with limited relevance to the assignments that I finally dared to write at the bottom page, "I know the answer. What is your question?"

Joseph Campbell, the distinguished professor at Sarah Lawrence College, in his remarkable interview with Bill Moyers on PBS discussing the Power of Myth, remarked that one of his students indignantly reproached him for giving too much reading. "I staggered under the weight of your weekly assignments. All professors assign heavy readings, and I am taking three other courses. How do you expect me to complete all this in a week?"

Joseph Campbell laughed and replied, "I am astonished you tried. You have the rest of your life to do the reading!" It is true. Not having to write papers for grades and to please my professors, I now relish reading my academic books.

In my first undergraduate class at Penn, I took a course in the Origins of Early Christianity. Why, out of all the Liberal Arts courses did I choose Early Christianity? I had already spoken to many Christian audiences, and I felt a need to find greater understanding of Christianity from a philosophical and historical perspective. Since my orientation was sociology, the subject of religious studies gave me a stronger basis to understand better how religious practices shape human behavior.

Many Christians and Jews would like to know each other better, not just as fellow-citizens and neighbors, but as persons of faith. To know each other better, one needs to look at the deeper questions about what concerns us most and how to build bridges that have separated Judaism and Christianity for so many centuries. Reading alone will never give you a really clear understanding of the faith of the other. It can only come as a result of a dialogue, by actively listening to the other from the depth of our convictions. It requires a willingness to entertain the possibility that change will take place in us, as well as in others, through mutual airing of thoughts.

As spiritual equals, the fruits of a dialogue can be remarkable. A dialogue in the traditional sense is a face-to-face meeting of minds in an open and friendly confrontation. It is a free discussion in an atmosphere of mutual respect and trust. In William Blake's words, the discovery of truth means a change in long-held convictions and clouded understanding. A person who never alters his opinion is like stagnant water that breeds reptiles of the mind.

To cite a true reconciliation, I will point to Pope John Paul II's historic gesture in visiting with Rome's Jewish community at its main synagogue in 1983. This was the first time in Catholic-Jewish relations that such a gesture ever took place. It signaled a desire for closer relations between the two faiths. It was stated that this short journey from the throne of Saint Peter to the central synagogue of Rome assured Pope John Paul II a special place of honor in modern Jewish history.

The Declaration of *Nostra Aetate* recalled the spiritual bond that links the Church to Judaism and called for mutual understanding and respect; it rejected both the deicide accusation and anti-Semitism. It urged theological and Biblical studies in a fraternal dialogue. It was a historical proclamation and perhaps the farthest leap into a new dimension in almost two millennia. What began in 1965 with the Second Vatican Council of the Catholic Church is considered a beginning rather than a final achievement. In the spirit of reconciliation, Christians and Jews have embarked on meaningful and productive dialogues.

I had the privilege to know the great Hebrew scholar, Professor Abraham Joshua Heschel, who had worked very closely with Pope John XXIII. Prof. Heschel remarked on furthering the Judeo-Christian dialogue, *"Respect for each other's faith is more than a political and social imperative. It is born of the insight that God is greater than religion; that faith is deeper than dogma; and that hatred, recrimination and persecution are irreligious."*

The desire to engage in a dialogue goes back to the beginning of time. In the Book of Genesis, God was looking for a dialogue with Adam. When Adam and Eve were banished from Eden, Adam went into hiding. He suddenly heard God calling, "Adam, where are you?" Why should God ask Adam where he was, since God knew where Adam was? It presented an enigmatic and perplexing question to Hebrew scholars because in Jewish thought, according to traditional interpretations of the event, what was important was not the sin of Adam and Eve, but what came after the sin. God wanted to start a dialogue with Adam by asking, "where are you?" and he wanted Adam to face up to the truth.

Religion was constructed not only as a means to inner peace through supplication, but also to tell people what is wrong and to take action. We learn from the Bible about many who took bold actions and stood up to oppression. Moses could have remained in the Pharaoh's palace. Jesus could have stayed in Galilee. Their conscience and valor changed the course of the world. Both found deep religious commitment that impelled them to sacrifice for the good of others. To find inner peace, you have to confront your conscience first, and sometimes this is painful. It demands introspection and honesty. Doing nothing is easier than doing something. The sacrament of reconciliation is ultimately a visible sign of inner grace.

I believe that in the scheme of things everyone has a specific mission in life, dictated by a higher power. This mission may not be revealed to us at first. In each situation, life presents a challenge. Perhaps we should not ask what is the meaning of life. Perhaps God has a plan that He does not want to reveal to us in simple terms so that each of us can find, recognize, and interpret our mission for ourselves. Discovering our mission means taking responsibility in faith and conscience and for our individual actions. Humans ultimately determine their own choices. We are given options. We make decisions, learn how to cope with rejection, learn how to be alone, and discover what ultimately leads us individually to finding inner peace.

I have learned to reconcile between good and evil, between beasts and humans. I have learned that it is important to teach the value of human life, and I have learned the value of ethics, morality, and religious freedom. To attain inner peace, one must have a clear conscience. We know that good and evil exist side by side. There exists an eternal duality, a tug-of-war between good and evil, and many allow themselves to be seduced by evil.

I have learned that when totalitarian governments impose laws that abandon individual and religious morals, it leads to human destruction of the soul and spirit. In a world that has no place for moral imperatives, the guilt of doing wrong doesn't exist. A world without a heart leads to a heart without a beat.

A few years ago when I was invited to speak to the faculty at Cornell University, I posed a rather provocative question. I asked them what constitutes higher education. Do we teach students morals and ethics or do universities produce technically competent barbarians interested only in their specific disciplines? The question originated from Dr. Franklin Littell, the distinguished scholar and Professor of Religion at Temple University, with whom I was privileged to engage in many fascinating discussions. I pointed out that in Nazi Germany, doctors and lawyers abandoned any notion of morality and made their own laws to suit the political environment. The crematoria were designed and built by people with Ph.D. degrees.

In light of past history and in search of reconciliation, probing deeper into one's soul and our willingness to understand other religions and cultures are absolutely essential to building a better world. No one religion can function in isolation. The eminent philosopher Martin Buber remarked, "Christians need more than ever to hear the voice of Jews who, perhaps more intensely than any other people, experienced the world's lack of redemption. For if Christians have a problem that forces them to ask: why, if the Messiah has come, is the world so evil? Jews also have a problem that forces them to ask why, with the world so evil, has the Messiah not come?"

There is an invisible power that reigns inside us. There is a splendid secret, a feeling of inner strength that compels us to press on with life when situations become difficult. It is easy to feel inner peace when all is well. But when we have to cope with stressful situations, we have to rely on the extra reserve and search for inner strength. You can never allow yourself the luxury of indulging in pessimistic thoughts. Shakespeare said: "Nothing is good or bad, but thinking makes it so." Positive thinking and feelings of inner peace act as a chain reaction, a chain reaction that's good for the soul.

In conclusion, I think that life could be compared to a carousel. It goes around in circles, stops at certain points, continues on, and goes around again. And at each point in our life, at each stop, we are faced with different challenges. We deal with angst and uncertainty, with joy and contentment. The secret is to be able to overcome and deal with adversity and go beyond it. The good and the difficult parts belong to that emotional symmetry which makes us function and achieve inner peace.

Chapter 12

Life's Journey—An Ongoing Process

Upon graduation from Temple University in May 1988, I continued to teach, but I also actively tried to find a reasonably well-paying, full-time position. A good friend suggested that I apply at a company with which he had professional dealings that dealt with experiential adult educational programs. I was advised that they were looking for a person who would specifically administer a new education program for members of a large labor union. I went for my first interview first in Philadelphia and then to meet the new Director in Washington, and I was invited to start my new job a week later.

And that is how I wound up becoming Director of the Educational Benefit Program for Local 1776, United Food and Commercial Workers' Health and Welfare Fund, a position I have continued to hold since 1990. In essence, this is a program that provides eligible union members, retail clerks in food and non-food stores the opportunity to pursue a post-secondary education: college, university, or vocational and technical training; toward the goal of upward economic mobility.

For six months I worked on developing and disseminating the education benefit, specifically geared to the union members of the Pennsylvania Liquor Control Board, which controls all retail liquor stores throughout the state. I would visit as many liquor stores as possible telling the clerks about the new and exciting union negotiated benefit that provided financial assistance toward higher education. I was able to generate quite a bit of publicity on television, over the radio, and in newspaper articles since the benefit was quite unique. The program in its limited capacity became quite successful.

Then, out of the clear blue sky, after six months I was fired. The acting director who oversaw the program before I was hired, for reasons that neither I nor anyone else could understand, became jealous of my obvious success and promptly informed me: "You don't know how to run a program." I called the President of the Union to inform him that I would no longer administer the benefit. I could hear real surprise in his voice when I spoke to him. I wanted to let him know of the development since he was also responsible for contracting the company that had hired me to run the program for the union.

The education program was Union President Wendell W. Young III's brainchild. He was deeply dedicated to bringing the opportunity for higher education to his union members, many of whom could not afford and had previously not entertained the idea of going to college. He had often pointed out that for many clerks, an educational benefit would represent their best hope of professional advancement. "Nobody goes to bed at night as a kid dreaming of becoming a retail clerk in a food store," he often said.

He asked me to see him at the union offices the next day. At that point, I had only met him three times. He knew what I was doing and how far the program had developed through the monthly reports I would send to the Union and the Board of Trustees. I met with Mr. Young and a few executive members.

A few months later the union terminated the relationship with the contracting company and hired me to take over the development and administration of the entire educational benefit, not just for the liquor store clerks for whom I was originally hired but also for food store clerks. Until then the program was handled as part of the claims department administered by the Health and Welfare Fund and lumped with all the other benefits.

When I took over the program in August 1990, working directly for UFCW Local 1776 Health and Welfare Fund, the numbers jumped within six months from a mere sixty-three members taking advantage of an educational benefit to 1,200. And by late 2004, the number of Union members who had improved their future prospects through vocational or college degrees had surged to thousands of members. I feel committed and dedicated to the program with a sense of pride.

In 1992, The University of Pennsylvania's College of General Studies was celebrating 100 years of lifelong education (1892-1992) and chose 100 CGS representatives as a cross-section of the student body over its centennial. I was one of the selected few from the class of 1984. Among the descriptions, it read: *"Nina Kaleska, '84 CGS, of Philadelphia, began college in 1981, thirty-six years after her primary school education ended with the Nazi occupation of her native Grodno, Poland. ....After her sons graduated from college, she applied to CGS to fulfill her dream of obtaining a formal education. She was advised that she needed to get her high school diploma. She studied for six weeks, took the required tests, and enrolled in her first class. A founding member of the CGS Alumni Group, she is now Director of Educational Programs for the United Food and Commercial Workers, Health and Welfare Fund in Plymouth Meeting, PA. She holds a Master's from Temple University..."*

In 1994, Union President Wendell W. Young III suggested that I submit our educational benefit program to the International Foundation of Employee Benefit Plans for the Creative Excellence Award. The Award was designed to recognize innovative programs that would spread awareness about unique ideas and concepts; programs honored had to have made a significant contribution to the employee benefits field. Entries were judged by members of the Foundation's Corporate Board and selected on specific criteria. Any program submitted for an award had to demonstrate creativity and newness, contain an important idea, and have potential for broad application.

Ron and Carla Harris

Ed and Jill Harris

Jeffrey Harris

Laura Harris

I wrote a detailed description of our program, and enclosed supporting documents and background material. Not expecting that our program might be chosen as one of the outstanding winners, I was pleasantly surprised to receive this notice from the Chief Executive Officer a few months later:

"I am pleased to inform you that the entry you submitted in the Creative Excellence in Benefits Award program has been selected to receive an award this year. It was chosen because the judges felt that it made a creative and innovative contribution to the field of employee benefits. Your program with three other winners will be recognized at an award luncheon to be held in conjunction with the International Foundation's 6th Annual Conference in San Francisco."

Out of hundreds of entries, I was very pleased that the United Food and Commercial Workers' Local 1776 Educational Benefit Program received the International Foundation Benefits Plans Excellence Award as the only educational program in the country. Our program was updated seven years later by the Foundation, and it was found to be still the only such unique benefit in the US. So much for not knowing how to run a program! What poetic justice.

I have come a long way from the sixteen-year old girl in June 1945 sitting alone on a bench in Prague on a warm afternoon, clutching a little bag with all her worldly possessions. The old worn white sweater I picked up in the repatriation center in Germany was draped over my shoulders. There was very little in that little bag except for two items that were very special to me: Lucien's love letter and his photograph. Somehow he became the embodiment of a semblance of humanity during a time of total inhumanity.

I have learned over the years that everything is relative. At that time, and in spite of the uncertainty of where life was going to take me, I was enjoying the freedom of not having guards standing over my head. I was not sure where I was going at that moment, but I was going somewhere and life looked promising. Prague's Vaclavske Namiesto was a nice place to wait for the next stop, not knowing where I would finally wind up and what life had in store.

I am no longer sitting on a bench alone although I find myself alone a great deal of the time, by choice. I keep remembering and recollecting, often with pain, often with amazement, with gratitude for many blessings, with sadness and nostalgia, the many unusual events that were and are part of my life and fate. Whenever I am involved in something worthwhile or important, I have the distinct feeling that my parents and sister are watching me somewhere in the outer world, and they approve of the way I have conducted my life. Perhaps this feeling is just my way and inner wish to share my life with my family I lost so many years ago… I derive a sense of pleasure and peace from this unexplained feeling.

As mentioned in one of my talks, there is a saying that there are three kinds of people: those who watch things happen; those who make things happen; and those who have no idea what happened. I watched how things have happened and, although the handwriting was clearly on the wall at that time, I had little understanding why people were ignoring the ominous clouds that were gathering over Europe. We know now that in Nazi Germany, the reign of terror began with meticulous planning of the master plan. It was methodically advanced, and the storm spread across many continents. At the end, the shattering thousand-year Reich Hitler envisioned in his demented glory lay crumbled, and with it laid millions of innocent lives: the price of one madman with a thousand accomplices. Doing something always takes more courage than doing nothing. We have a parallel today, and equanimity in the face of unspeakable evil is not enough to express profound indignation… something the United Nations seems to do so well.

I was too young at that time to know how to make things happen and to make a difference for positive changes. But, having forged through many streams and obstacles, I have accepted over the years the bad and the good with a positive attitude and optimistic outlook. I thank my beloved parents, Rachil and Chaim Zelik Kalecki, who transmitted to me this genetic trait. Without a positive attitude and optimism, I could not have made it over the years. Even at an early age, my parents have instilled in me the importance of the value of education and the importance of being honest. They gave me a special gift for which I am eternally grateful.

I have come to recognize that the world owes you very little except what you are willing to contribute back to it. By over-coming many obstacles I have, with deliberate passion, embraced the desire to conquer difficult circumstances. I know what happened, and I have attempted to share some of my knowledge with those who were interested in hearing what I have to impart.

Like a carousel, life stops at certain points, some good and some bad, but it keeps on spinning until it reaches the next stop. Let's see where it will take me next. My life has been fragment-ed, and often one incident had nothing to do with another. I suppose the art of living is the ability to connect the fragments in some semblance, and my ability to take an optimistic approach helped me to build a reservoir of psychological resilience. I don't think I could have survived without it. There is still so much to learn and accomplish. Life is a heck of an adventure.